# Freemasonry

www.pocketessentials.com

Other Pocket Essentials by Giles Morgan:

*Byzantium*
*The Holy Grail*
*St George*

# Freemasonry

GILES MORGAN

**POCKET ESSENTIALS**

This edition published in 2007 by Pocket Essentials
P.O.Box 394, Harpenden, Herts, AL5 1XJ
www.pocketessentials.com

A CIP catalogue record for this book is available from the British Library.

ISBN 10: 1 904048 87 0
ISBN 13: 978 1 904048 87 9

2 4 6 8 10 9 7 5 3 1

Typeset by Avocet Typeset, Chilton, Aylesbury, Bucks
Printed by J. H. Haynes & Co Ltd., Sparkford

# Contents

# Introduction

Freemasonry is a topic that polarises opinion. Much of the controversy which surrounds the subject has centred on the perception that Freemasons represent a secret society with sinister aims and objectives that has wielded a powerful but unseen influence through history. Its many critics have labelled it as an organisation that is variously corrupt, manipulative, self-serving and even satanic. Those who have attempted to defend the reputation of Freemasonry have often pointed out that it can be more realistically regarded as not so much a secret society as a fraternal society that has its own secrets. Advocates of Freemasonry argue that the secrecy surrounding its rituals and meetings is mainly limited to codes of recognition within what its members call the 'Craft'.

Freemasonry is a global phenomenon and examples of Masonic-type groups can be found throughout the world. Many view Freemasonry as holding high moral aims and ideals. Membership is potentially open to anyone over the age of 21 with a belief in a supreme being. However, in order to become a Freemason, candidates must be nominated and vetted by existing Freemasons. For the critics of Freemasonry this process is indicative of the elitism and protectionism that is the true nature of the order.

Perhaps one of the most puzzling and perplexing aspects of Freemasonry is the way in which it defines itself. During initiation ceremonies candidates are commonly asked the ritual question, 'What is Freemasonry?' The answer generally given is, 'A peculiar system of morality, veiled in allegory and illustrated by symbols'. Freemasonry also states that its three grand founding principles are 'brotherly love, relief and truth'. Entrants to Masonic societies are very often required to progress through a series of ceremonies in which the mysteries of the Craft are revealed to them before they reach the rank of Master Mason. The circumstances and content of these rituals have led many, both within and outside Freemasonry, to question how they began and what meanings they contain.

It is often claimed that Freemasonry is the oldest surviving secret society in the world and the numerous beliefs about its beginnings seem to point towards ancient and esoteric origins. The origins of Freemasonry are obscure and uncertain but a body of different theories has emerged in an attempt to answer the seemingly fundamental and basic question of how the Craft began. It has been variously argued that it derives from the practices of medieval stonemasons, that it dates to events surrounding the construction of the Temple of

Solomon and that it is connected to ancient Mystery Cults. One of the major and often disputed claims made for Freemasonry is that it is directly linked to the Knights Templar. Best-selling books *The Holy Blood and the Holy Grail* and more recently Dan Brown's *The Da Vinci Code* have linked Freemasonry to a supposed secret order known as the Priory of Sion which is the guardian of the true nature of the Holy Grail. Freemasonry also features heavily in Brown's novels *Angels and Demons* and *The Solomon Key*.

The earliest written documentary evidence of Freemasonry dates mainly from the sixteenth century although some have claimed references to it can be found in older texts. The creation of the Grand Lodge of England in 1717 is often seen as a major turning point or event in the history of Freemasonry as the order became more visible to a wider public for the first time. It has been argued that Freemasonry has played an important role in the shaping of American society and it is known that a number of key figures in American history such as George Washington and Benjamin Franklin were themselves Freemasons.

Some have claimed that Freemasonry also influenced the French Revolution and draw parallels between the slogan 'Liberty, Equality, Fraternity' and its own three grand founding principles. On a more sinister level it has been claimed in recent years that the Victorian serial killer Jack the Ripper was a Freemason and the brotherhood has been linked to organised crime. However, it is perhaps less well known that many thousands of Freemasons were amongst those persecuted and killed by the Nazis during the Second World War. Adolf Hitler attacked the Freemasons in *Mein Kampf* and considered them to be enemies of the Nazi party. Its members were barred from holding public office and arrested and interned in concentration camps as political prisoners.

In more recent times Masonic-type groups such as P2 in Italy have been involved in corruption scandals that have perpetuated the image of Freemasonry as a secretive and self-serving network involved in nefarious activities. Conversely, many Freemasons have pointed to their charitable work, collecting money for a number of causes, and their tradition of scholarly research and education as important and positive aspects of their organisations. Freemasonry can boast many famous and distinguished members throughout its history, ranging from Mozart and Sir Isaac Newton to Sir Winston Churchill and Buzz Aldrin in the twentieth century. Freemasonry has played an important and often little-known role in the shaping of Western culture and, in this sense at least, its development can credibly be claimed to represent something of a secret history.

# What is Freemasonry?

Attempting to answer the basic question of what Freemasonry actually is and the associated one of how it originated has proved a surprisingly complex and difficult task for both Masons and non-Masons alike. In 1984, following a flurry of interest in the Brotherhood, a leaflet was produced by Freemasons and issued by a group with the slightly Pythonesque title of the 'Board of General Purposes'. The leaflet, entitled *What Is Freemasonry?*, describes Freemasonry as:

> one of the world's oldest secular fraternal societies... a society of men concerned with spiritual values. Its members are taught its precepts by a series of ritual dramas, which follow ancient forms and use stonemason's customs and tools as allegorical guides.
>
> (*The Craft*, John Hamill, p.12).

The simplest definition of Freemasonry then is that it is a fraternal organisation found in one form or another in a wide and varied range of countries around the world.

However, Freemasonry can also be regarded as a

secret society in that many of the inner workings of the organisation are not revealed to the general public. Freemasons aim to improve themselves by learning moral and spiritual lessons taught within the fraternity, not only to develop and benefit their own characters, but also in order to contribute in positive ways to the fraternity and to wider society.

Its members traditionally share a moral code and value system with a belief in a single Supreme Being or deity. It is essential that prospective Masons have a belief in a Supreme Being or deity in order to pursue a course of spiritual growth. Providing that this criterion is met, the candidate is free to adhere to more or less any religion that they choose. One of the tenets of Freemasonry is that its members are at liberty to follow their own separate beliefs but it safeguards this freedom by forbidding religious discussion within its meetings. Similarly, discussion of political issues is prohibited within Masonic meetings in order to promote unity and harmony amongst its members. As we shall see, this has not always been the case but, none the less, it is an ideal that is central to Freemasonry.

The vast majority of Freemasons belong to what is called 'Craft' or 'Blue Lodge' Freemasonry. Its members usually meet together under the guidance and leadership of a Worshipful Master and other Masonic officials at a local level. The officers of the lodge, led by the Worshipful Master, will initiate new members and deal with issues relevant to the lodge or local area. An important aspect of Freemasonry is that its members should contribute actively towards charitable and worthwhile causes. There are three levels or ranks within Craft Masonry: the Entered Apprentice referred to as the first degree; the Fellowcraft which is the second degree; and the third degree of Master Mason.

It is also important to recognise that Freemasonry cannot be regarded as one coherent and single body. Rather Freemasonry today is the culmination of differing historical traditions and trends that will be discussed in greater detail in later chapters. Individual Masonic Lodges are governed by a Grand Lodge that varies from territory to territory. For example in Britain there are different Grand Lodges for each country within the United Kingdom. English Masonry is presided over by the United Grand Lodge of England whilst the Grand Lodge of Ireland and the Grand Lodge of Scotland preside over their member's activities. The central image or symbol around which Freemasonry is organised and teaches its spiritual and moral lessons to Masons is the building of the Temple of Solomon. Just as the Temple was intended to be perfect in its form and function in providing an earthly home for God, so Masons are taught that they must strive to perfect themselves and thus contribute to wider society.

## Masonic Principles

The basic principles on which Freemasonry is said to be based and which are intended to inform the thoughts and actions of Masons are Brotherly Love, Relief and Truth. The principle of Brotherly Love emphasises tolerance and mutual respect and working towards a harmonious and productive society. Relief is widely interpreted as offering assistance and aid to those who require it within society through charitable donations and aid. The principle of Truth requires that a Mason should strive to attain high moral standards and aim to fulfil his responsibilities as a Mason and as a citizen.

Freemasonry instructs its members through a series of symbolic and allegorical moral lessons that are described as degrees. It has been argued that these Masonic principles played a major part in determining the idealised qualities and beliefs upon which the Constitution of the United States of America is claimed to have been founded. As we shall see, the Masonic principles of Brotherly Love, Relief and Truth also had a considerable influence upon the ideals of the French Revolution, one which can be recognised in the famous Republican rallying call of 'Liberty, Equality, Fraternity'.

## Masonic Lodges

A Masonic lodge is the term given to a group of Masons and does not denote the meeting place in which they attend. The lodge rooms where Masons meet may vary in size or relative grandeur but they do share a core set of characteristics. Within Freemasonry it is important that the room in which the lodge meets should have an alignment running from east to west. Essentially, and as we shall discover significantly, the Worshipful Master is always seated in the East corner of the lodge room. Lodge members are seated on benches along the south and north walls that are themselves split into east and west groupings. One of the most distinctive and recognisable characteristics of the lodge room is usually the floor upon which a black and white chequered pattern of squares features prominently either as a carpet, tiles or mosaic. Conversely the ceiling often has a depiction of the sun or the heavens. On a practical level the lodge will generally have its warrant from its Grand Lodge visible, that demonstrates its right to assemble and function as a Masonic lodge.

The personnel at the core of a lodge hold seven positions; the Tyler, the Inner Guard, the Junior Deacon, the Senior Deacon, the Junior Warden, the Senior Warden and the Worshipful Master. The Tyler has the role of standing outside the doors that lead into the lodge and is required to prevent any unlawful entry into the inner chamber and to make sure that the business of the lodge is not being overheard by outsiders. The Tyler also greets all those entering the lodge and must ensure that Masons are properly dressed (usually in black suits with black ties and white shirts) before allowing them entry to the lodge room. Traditionally the Tyler stood guard with a ceremonial sword to stop eavesdropping or forced entry to the lodge. The Tyler's Sword often has a wavy blade because, in the Book of Genesis, a flaming sword was placed in the east of the Garden of Eden to guard the Tree of Life.

The Inner Guard performs the same role as the Tyler but within the lodge room. Ceremonially, the Inner Guard will check that the Tyler is performing his duties by knocking on the door of the lodge to which the Tyler must reply by knocking the outside of the door.

Initiates are met within the lodge by the Inner Guard who then escorts them to meet the Junior Deacon. The Junior Deacon helps candidates to prepare for cere-monies of initiation and monitors those who enter and leave the room during a lodge session. He must ensure that any that do leave or enter do so only with the permission of the Senior Deacon or Worshipful Master. He carries messages on behalf of the Senior Deacon.

The Senior Deacon performs the same function for the Worshipful Master and has responsibility for the introduction of Masons from other lodges to members of his own. Within the lodge the Senior Deacon plays a significant part in initiation ceremonies, leading candi-dates and participating in ritual speeches. The Senior Deacon will generally progress within the hierarchy of the lodge and so must undergo training to prepare him for his next role in a 'lodge of instruction'. The role of the Junior Warden is to arrange the business of the lodge in terms of liaising with visitors from other lodges and (importantly) of covering the duties of the Senior Warden and Worshipful Master if they are absent. The Senior Warden is second in command and must be able both to help the Worshipful Master and to take his place in his absence and prepare for his own ascension to that role.

The Worshipful Master is the highest-ranking position within a lodge and he must govern its business and ceremonies and play a central part in its rituals. The Worshipful Master is the most important point of contact between the lodge and its respective Governing Grand Lodge. The Worshipful Master is responsible for the opening and closing of lodge sessions and for maintaining order and appropriate behaviour within it.

There are a number of other non-ceremonial officers who operate within the framework of the lodge. Typically there would be around eight such officers although, in some lodges, there are more. The least senior of these is the Junior Steward and his primary purpose is not to participate in the rituals and ceremonies of the lodge but to assist with lodge activities before sessions are opened and when they are closed. The Junior Steward would provide assistance to the Senior Steward and help the Junior Warden with the provision of food and drink. Those serving as Junior Steward are seen as gaining experience and knowledge in order to progress within the framework of the lodge. The Senior Steward also plays an important role during meals, checking that everything is running smoothly whilst also providing support and assistance to the lodge officers. All lodge meetings begin and end with prayer and it is the responsibility of the Chaplain to lead the lodge in this activity. He is also responsible for the safekeeping of the Volume of the Sacred Law. The Chaplain must also attend the funerals of Masons where he would be expected to say prayers for the deceased.

Contact between the lodge and its members is the responsibility of the Almoner. It falls to the Almoner to alert lodge members to any of their number who may need assistance due to ill health. Donations and links to external charities are maintained by the Charity Steward and he coordinates charitable fundraising within the lodge. The financial affairs of the lodge are the preserve of the Treasurer who is expected to maintain exact and honest records of the income and outflow of the lodge's monies. The Worshipful Master will also receive help and assistance from the Immediate Past Master who will be the predecessor of the current master. The administrative needs of the lodge are largely met by the Secretary who deals with paperwork generated through meetings and links with other lodges. The Secretary is responsible for maintaining an accurate and up-to-date list of lodge members.

## Regularity

Freemasonry today is often viewed as a homogenous single global entity but, in reality, there are many different Masonic organisations that have developed over time and through diverse circumstances. An important issue to arise from this is the question of regularity. Put simply, the Grand Lodge of a particular territory or jurisdiction must give its approval for a lodge to be considered 'regular'.

There is an obvious need for Freemasonry to monitor both its own activities and any potentially fraudulent organisations claiming an unjustifiable link with the fraternity. Together with the central principles on which Freemasonry is said to be founded, the question of regularity and whether a lodge is recognised or not is widely regarded as one of the fundamental issues of Freemasonry. Participating in irregular lodges would be punishable by expulsion from Freemasonry and so, of course, is perceived as an issue of some considerable gravity. Different Grand Lodges are described as being 'in amity' when they are in a state of mutual recognition and members are permitted to interact officially at lodge level.

## The First Degree

In order to become a Mason, individuals must fulfil a number of basic requirements. They are usually recommended for membership by other Masons and must be of legal age. (Depending on the jurisdiction, that may be 18 or 21 years of age.) They must be without criminal convictions and be observed to be of good moral character. It is often stated that they should be 'free-born', an archaic survival that would originally have meant that they were not slaves. Importantly, they must also hold a belief in a single Supreme Being with an associated belief in an afterlife. On this point Freemasonry claims to be non-specific and would be open to any monotheistic religion such as Christianity or Islam. The suitability of candidates is voted on by a secret ballot of the lodge to which they are attempting to gain entry. In order to be successfully accepted all members of the lodge must agree to the suitability of the candidate. Traditionally, during the vote, black and white balls (or sometimes cubes) are used to register votes. A white ball signifies a 'yes' vote and a black ball registers a 'no'. The common term of 'blackballing' someone (usually in connection with membership of an organisation) is thought to derive from this Masonic process.

As has already been mentioned, Freemasonry is most commonly divided into what is known as the 'Three Degrees' or 'level' of Mason. Many other higher levels within Freemasonry can be achieved but, for the vast rank and file of the Brotherhood, these Three Degrees are the norm. The first degree or step in Freemasonry is that of the 'Entered Apprentice', the second degree is known as 'Fellowcraft' and the third degree is that of 'Master Mason'. The first degree of the Entered Apprentice is marked by a ceremony known as the 'Rite of Destitution' in which initiates symbolically take their first step into the world of Freemasonry. Initiates are required to wear simple clothes such as white cotton trousers and a shirt provided for the occasion that are intended to focus their attention on their inner selves rather than on worldly status or wealth. They are typically blindfolded or 'hoodwinked' and all money and metal objects on their person are removed. One foot is fitted with a slipper, a state that is referred to as being 'slipshod'. Each initiate has his left leg bared to the knee and his left breast exposed. A rope or hangman's noose called a cable tow is fitted loosely around his neck and a sword or dagger is held to his left breast.

After the guard has knocked on the door of the Temple, the candidate is led into the room. The initiate undertakes a vow of secrecy during the ceremony and he is led by the cable tow around the floor of the Temple. The reasons for the candidate being led around the Temple in this way are a mixture of practical and metaphorical concerns. Being led around the Temple in a system of ritual patterns gives the other members of the lodge the opportunity to see the candidate and that he is ready to undertake this next phase of his development within Freemasonry. It also has symbolic value. The candidate can be imagined as undergoing the process of threading his way through a labyrinth and being orientated within the world of Freemasonry. He is referred to as 'a poor candidate in a state of darkness' and introduced to the Lodge.

During this symbolic ritual the hoodwinked apprentice asks to be shown 'the light' and is brought before the Worshipful Master who stands at the altar. When the blindfold is removed the candidate's attention is drawn to what are referred to as the 'Great Lights' of Freemasonry that have been laid upon the altar. These include the volume of sacred law, which is typically the Bible, but could be another text related to the candidate's faith system, the Square and the Compasses. The Bible is the guide by which Masons should live their lives whilst the square symbolises truth and the compasses represent knowledge and expertise.

It is interesting to note how many concepts and phrases that are commonly in use today derive from Freemasonry and its attendant imagery. For example, an individual who is believed to be reliable, honest and trustworthy may be described as a 'four-square fellow' or equally as being 'on the level'. Similarly, a commitment or deal might be described as being 'fair and square'. As we shall also see, people commonly describe an individual who has been put through a rigorous or testing ordeal of some kind as having been subjected to or given 'the third degree', a reflection of the gravity and seriousness which the process of becoming a Master Mason is perceived to have.

## Masonic Aprons

Candidates take a solemn oath of allegiance at the altar that lays out what their fellow Masons expect from them and what their responsibilities and status within the lodge are. Because the oath is sworn at the altar in the presence of the Bible or other sacred text, it is seen as a sacred promise sworn within the sight of God. At the next stage of the first degree ceremony the initiate will be presented with a white apron made from lambskin. This symbolises the innocence of the entered apprentice. (Different degrees within Freemasonry are represented by different apron designs.) It is expected that the entered apprentice will fulfil his duties to the Brotherhood and society and conduct himself in a moral and upright manner.

Like the square and the compasses, the apron is thought by some to derive from the time when groups of working stonemasons organised themselves into fraternal groups and all three items had a practical application. These stonemasons, who are credited with building the great cathedrals and abbeys of the Middle Ages, are referred to as 'operative' freemasons. Over time Freemasonry developed into what is referred to as a 'speculative' form in that it became increasingly open to, and dominated by, individuals who did not actually work as masons. The role of the apron within modern Freemasonry is symbolic and modern Masons see much of their work as inner activity and personal development rather than the physical labour of the old stonemasons. The white apron made from lambskin also relates to the story of the building of the Temple of King Solomon and the unlawful killing of its chief architect Hiram Abiff that is central to the allegorical lessons that Freemasonry teaches to Masons and which is discussed in greater detail in Chapter Two.

## Working Tools

When the candidate has been presented with his apron the next phase of his initiation into the world of Freemasonry involves presenting him with the 'working tools' of the Entered Apprentice. These are actual builders' tools of the kind that, it is said, medieval apprentice stonemasons would have used but, in this instance, their value is symbolic rather than actual. The Entered Apprentice is shown a ruler called a 24-inch gauge and a stonemason's hammer known as the common gavel. The symbolism of the 24-inch gauge, which is used to take measurements, is that it folds up into three sections. The apprentice is informed that the gauge represents an individual day and that the way it divides into three sections illustrates the use that Masons should make of their time. Within one eight-hour section Masons should carry out their work or job, they should spend a further eight hours devoting themselves to their religion, improving themselves and performing charitable works and the remaining eight hours resting themselves through sleep. Candidates are then introduced to the symbolism of the hammer or common gavel and it is explained that they should work on themselves and their own characters. Just as the stonemason's hammer would be used to refine and shape stone, the apprentices must try to rid themselves of behaviour or unwanted characteristics in refining and improving their moral worth as Masons.

## The Immovable Jewels

During the next phase of the ceremony the apprentice Mason is led to stand in the north-eastern corner of the lodge. The symbolism of placing the candidate in this area of the room is that it is traditional to lay the first stone of a building in the north-east corner and it is referred to as the cornerstone. Therefore the apprentice is symbolically creating the basis for the building of his own spiritual temple through Freemasonry.

Significantly the Worshipful Master sits in the east because this is believed to be the place of light, the point from which the sun rises, whilst the north is a point of darkness for Masons. The candidate is moving towards the light of instruction and the attainment of wisdom is represented by the presence of the Worshipful Master.

The apprentice is shown the three pillars that support the lodge and which symbolise wisdom, strength and beauty. In Masonic lore the three pillars also represent the three Grand Masters on which Freemasonry is based: King Solomon, Hiram, King of Tyre and the Master Builder, Hiram Abiff. The three pillars are shown to be linked to the roles of the three Lesser Lights of the lodge that are the persons of the Worshipful Master, Senior Warden and the Junior Warden. The apprentice will also be shown the Immovable Jewels of the lodge: the square, the level and the plumb line. The square symbolises morality, the level represents equality and the plumb line stands for goodness.

## The Movable Jewels

The apprentice will also be shown the so-called Movable Jewels: the rough ashlar, the perfect ashlar and the trestleboard. An ashlar is a square-cut stone used in building and appears here in rough-hewn form and also in a perfected and prepared state. The trestleboard would, in building work, have been used to hold the plans of an architect. Within the symbolism of Freemasonry, the rough ashlar represents the spiritual state of the Entered Apprentice, the perfect ashlar corresponds to the Fellowcraft Mason and the trestleboard refers to the work that a Master Mason should undertake in building a spiritual temple within himself. Tracing boards are another traditional tool used within Freemasonry for teaching and educating its members. They often consist of a colourful series of symbols and images that to non-Masons can appaear surreal and bizarre but which have philosophical and instructional meaning to Masons. They take their name from the tracing boards used by medieval stonemasons to cut stone to specific shapes and dimensions.

# The Fellowcraft and the Master Mason

## The Second Degree

The next stage in the development of a Mason is the ceremony of the second degree where he becomes what is referred to as a 'Fellowcraft Freemason'. On a symbolic level the candidate is seen to be spiritually 'coming of age' and entering the mature, adult phase of his Masonic development. Initially, the candidate enters the Temple wearing the white lambskin apron that symbolises his status as Entered Apprentice. He is asked a series of ritual questions and provides answers to these. Upon completion of this part of the ceremony the candidate must leave the Temple to don the same simple costume that was required for the ritual of the first degree and re-enters the Temple with his left leg bare and his shirt pulled back from his right breast.

Just as the ceremony of the Entered Apprentice features specific working tools of symbolic value, so the ritual induction to the level of Fellowcraft Mason is accompanied by an introduction to further such implements. The working tools shown to the Fellowcraft

Mason are described as the three immovable jewels of the lodge. As previously mentioned, they consist of the square, the level and the plumb line. The symbolism of the square within Freemasonry is that its two sides create a perfect right angle. In order to build a strong and stable wall a builder or mason must ensure that it stands completely upright forming a 90-degree angle with the ground.

The importance of this image and idea within Freemasonry is that a Mason must strive to ensure that his behaviour and conduct are similarly upright and without deviation. Without maintaining this high standard the Mason risks a metaphorical fall. The level teaches Masons that, regardless of the circumstances of our birth, we are all equal within the sight of God and must work to improve ourselves both in the physical, material world and in terms of spiritual and inner development. The plumb line is a Masonic working tool that emphasises the importance of fair play and treating others equally and acts as a symbol of equal justice for all untainted by unworthy bias.

## The Winding Staircase

The symbolism of the winding staircase is central to the second degree of Fellowcraft Masonry. This image is taken from the architectural design that Freemasons believe that the Temple of Solomon followed. During the ritual of the first degree the ceremony symbolically takes place on the ground floor of King Solomon's Temple. To advance to the next degree the apprentice Mason must symbolically ascend by the winding staircase to the Middle Chamber of the Temple. The image of stairs or ladders or even mountains within the symbolic language of Freemasonry is a common one and denotes the ascension of Masons within the Brotherhood. To reach the second degree within Freemasonry means that the Mason is entitled to what is known as increased wages. These wages are symbolic and are represented in the form of corn, wine and oil.

The symbolism of ascension within Freemasonry draws on the biblical story of Jacob's Ladder. During a dream Jacob saw a ladder that connected the Earth with Heaven, and God told him that the Jewish people would be given the land that stretched from the River Euphrates to the south-west. As a monument to the dream, Jacob took the stone upon which he had laid his head whilst asleep and set it upright. He dedicated the stone to God by pouring oil upon it. The numbers three and seven are significant within Freemasonry. There are, of course, three degrees within Blue Lodge Masonry, the three principles of Brotherly Love, Relief and Truth upon which Freemasonry is founded; there are three principal officers within a lodge and there are the three virtues of faith, hope and charity that lead to heaven. The seven liberal arts and sciences are symbolised by seven steps on the winding staircase. The formulation of the seven liberal arts and sciences can be dated to the fourth century AD and many Christian thinkers believed that to gain mastery of them was a means of achieving a greater understanding of God. They are generally said to be the subjects of rhetoric, grammar, geometry, music, mathematics, astronomy and logic.

Another central image to the second degree ceremony is that of the two pillars that appear at the entrance to all Masonic lodges which are a reference to the pillars that were set at the entrance to King Solomon's Temple. The initiate is informed that they represent strength and establishment and signify control and power within the lodge. It has also been argued that the image of the two pillars at the entrance to the Temple originated with the biblical account of the Pillar of Cloud and the Pillar of Fire that led the Israelites to the Promised Land. From the eighteenth century many lodges chose to place globes on top of the pillars and, although there is no evidence available to prove this point, some have claimed that such spheres surmounted the pillars of the Temple of Solomon. They are sometimes said to symbolise the two different spheres of earth and heaven. However, in some lodges, the globes were displayed on tripods close to the seat of the Worshipful Master.

When the Fellowcraft reaches the middle chamber of the Temple he is due the previously mentioned wages of corn, wine and oil. Their symbolic value is that they represent spiritual and mental wealth and plenty. Corn is, of course, symbolic of sustenance since wheat is used to create bread, one of the basic foodstuffs upon which we all depend. Wheat also appears in Masonic imagery woven into the shape of a cornucopia, often overflowing with fruit and berries. The Senior Steward of a lodge, who has a non-ceremonial role, is responsible for refreshment in the form of food and drink during meetings and commonly wears an emblem or badge, described by Masons as 'jewels' and featuring the motif of a cornucopia set between the points of the Masonic Compass. Wine denotes peace and good health and, in a Christian context, is arguably linked to the ceremony of the Eucharist. Oil is believed to symbolise happiness and joy. For the Mason receiving these wages, they represent a just reward for leading a good life. The wages within Masonic lore derive from the 'wages' or tithes that King Solomon paid the King of Tyre for the help he provided, in the form of builders and materials, for the construction of the Temple.

## The Third Degree

During the ceremony of the third degree, when the Fellowcraft Mason is said to achieve the 'sublime' status of becoming a Master Mason, the candidate is required to enact the role of the Grand Master of the building of the Temple of Solomon, Hiram Abiff. Through this drama the candidate undergoes a figurative death, burial and resurrection. The Worshipful Master of the lodge narrates the story of Hiram Abiff, a legend that is central to Masonic ceremony, lore and culture. As we shall see in later chapters, the theme of resurrection can be found in many cultures and legends and has fuelled considerable speculation about the origins of Freemasonry. In the story that is related to the candidate by the Worshipful Master it is said that the Grand Master Hiram Abiff, who was the principal architect of the Temple of Solomon, was murdered shortly before its completion. As a Grand Master Hiram Abiff was in possession of the 'genuine secrets of a Master Mason' and it is said that 15 Fellowcraft Masons junior to him formulated a conspiracy to extract those secrets from him unlawfully.

On the night before they planned to demand the secrets from Hiram Abiff, twelve of the fifteen Fellowcraft abandoned their disreputable intentions but the remaining three remained determined to confront their Grand Master. The three Fellowcraft stationed themselves at the east, south and west gates of the Temple of Solomon whilst Hiram Abiff was inside praying to the 'Most High' at the hour of 'high twelve'. When Hiram attempted to leave the Temple through the south gate he was confronted by one of these lawless 'ruffians' who demanded that he provide him with the secrets of a Master Mason and threatened to kill him if he did not supply the information. Hiram replied that only three individuals knew those secrets and that he could not impart them without the agreement of the other two. The Grand Master offered words of encouragement to the Fellowcraft, suggesting that, in time and with his own personal development, he would be able to gain those secrets lawfully. However, he, Hiram, could not reveal them before that time because of the 'sacred trust' that his position involved even if it meant his own death. Greatly angered, the Fellowcraft struck a blow at Hiram's forehead that actually hit his right temple. The blow knocked Hiram down onto his left knee. Staggering back to his feet, Hiram attempted to leave the Temple through the west gate but was met by the second ruffian who made the same demand as the first. Once again Hiram refused to give up the secrets of a Master Mason and the man struck him a blow with a level on his left temple that, this time, drove him down onto his right knee.

Injured and bleeding, the Grand Master finally attempted to leave through the east gate of the Temple where he was confronted by the third ruffian who repeated the demands of his companions. Hiram stayed resolute in his determination to fulfil his obligation not to reveal those secrets entrusted to him and refused to answer. The Fellowcraft then struck him viciously in the centre of the forehead with a heavy stone maul that killed him instantly and the body of the Grand Master lay sprawled on the floor of the Temple.

After the murder of Hiram Abiff, when the various workmen who had participated in the construction of the Temple met together, it was noticed that three of their number were missing. At this point the 12 Fellowcraft who had originally plotted against Hiram

Abiff confessed the conspiracy to King Solomon and revealed all that had been planned. Greatly concerned by the absence of the Master Mason in light of what had been revealed King Solomon ordered that 15 Fellowcraft begin a search for him to determine whether or not he had been slain by the remaining three conspirators.

A date was agreed that they should return to Jerusalem and the men joined themselves into three Lodges and set out on their search from the three gates of the Temple. One group searched without any success at all and returned without answers. The second made an important discovery when one of their number, who was resting on the ground after searching for the Master Mason, dislodged a shrub from the ground and found that the earth in which it grew was loose and came away easily. Investigating further, they discovered the hastily buried body of Hiram Abiff. They then recovered the body but marked the place of its burial by sticking a sprig of acacia near where the head of the Grand Master had lain. (It is interesting to note that in Middle Eastern cultures the acacia is associated with such themes as rebirth and new growth because it is an evergreen plant. Some traditions maintain that the crown of thorns that Jesus was forced to wear at the crucifixion was made from acacia.) Returning swiftly to Jerusalem, they informed King Solomon of their unhappy find. King Solomon ordered that they should return to the site of the burial and create a sepulchre

for Hiram Abiff that reflected his status and importance. He also informed the men that, because of the
death of Hiram Abiff, the secrets of a Master Mason
were now lost.

The third lodge of Fellowcraft had been searching
westwards and had arrived in Joppa and happened upon
the three disgraced murderers. A member of the group
heard one of the murderers whose name was Jubela
wailing that he would rather have had his throat cut and
his tongue torn out by its root and buried in the sand a
cable length from the shore where the tide passes twice
in the course of a day than to be involved in the murder
of Hiram Abiff. The second villain Jubelo cried that he
would rather have his heart ripped out from his chest
and given to the vultures than to have played his part in
the killing of the Master Mason. The third villain
Jubelum declared that because he had struck the blow
that killed Hiram Abiff he would rather that his body be
cut into two parts and those separate parts be taken
north and south and his bowels burnt to ashes and
thrown to the four winds than that he be guilty of the
murder of the Master Mason. The searching Fellowcraft
who heard the lamenting killers took them prisoner and
marched them back to Jerusalem where they confessed
their guilt to King Solomon. As punishment for their
crime they were all sentenced to the grisly deaths for
which they had yearned. In Masonic lore the three
murderers of Hiram Abiff are referred to as the Juwes,
pronounced 'Joo-ees'. Hiram was said to have been

reburied close to the Temple and the Fellowcraft who had searched for him attended the funeral wearing white gloves and aprons that served as tokens or symbols of their innocence.

During the ceremony that echoes this story, the initiate is described as being raised to the sublime degree of a Master Mason. In the course of the ritual the candidate is actually physically raised from the floor by his fellow Masons.

## The Master Mason

The working tools of the degree of the Master Mason are the skirret, pencil and the compass. A skirret is a pointed building tool that can be set in the ground and used to plan a true line from which to work. This, of course, is metaphorically extended to the behaviour and deportment of Master Masons who should use the religious teachings of their own faith system in tandem with the standards required of them by Freemasonry. The symbolism of the pencil lies in the fact that, whilst an architect or builder can use it in planning a structure, it also serves to record the actions of individuals.

The Master Mason must bear in mind that his actions will be judged by his fellow Masons and by God. The significance of the compass is that, as an instrument, it is used to determine calculations to a high standard and thus it represents the role of the Supreme Being as the ultimate judge of mankind. The ceremony of becoming a Master Mason can be seen as representing the third phase of human life.

The Entered Apprentice relates symbolically to childhood and beginnings and the Fellowcraft symbolises adulthood and 'coming of age'. The ritual of the Master Mason equates to old age and the gaining of experience and wisdom, together with a realisation of our own mortality but one accompanied by the comfort of belief in the immortality of the human soul.

The ceremony of the third degree of the Master Mason also includes a number of other images and motifs whose symbolic significance is explained to the initiate by the Worshipful Master. A pot of incense represents an individual whose heart is pure and a worthy sacrifice to offer to God. The Mason is told that, just as the incense pot glows and burns with internal heat, so should our hearts in gratitude to God for our lives and for such blessings that have been bestowed upon us. The image of the beehive is a common one in Freemasonry and the Mason is instructed that it represents the theme of hard work and industry and the importance of dedication to our labours. Importantly, the motif of the beehive is also a reminder to Masons that they should work to provide charity, relief and help to those in need and emphasises that this is particularly the case if it is within our power to do so.

The emblem of the Book of Constitutions that is guarded by the Tyler's sword symbolises the importance of being perpetually aware of our actions and thoughts.

Masons are taught to be cautious in discussing the private matters of Freemasonry and to be careful of what they say or reveal to others, particularly those who are hostile to Freemasonry. The symbol of the naked heart with a sword being pointed toward it represents divine justice that knows all and sees all of our actions and will reward or punish us on the basis of these. The Anchor and the Ark draws on the story of Noah and symbolises a life that is well grounded. By living virtuous and upright lives Masons will be protected by the safety and reward of a metaphorical ark where the soul will be rewarded after death.

The candidate is also taught to regard Pythagoras's theorem, referred to as the 47th problem of Euclid. The significance of this within the ritual is to remind the Mason to understand and appreciate the importance of science and the arts. The Worshipful Master will ask the candidate to regard the emblem of the hourglass and to recognise that, just as the sand runs quickly through it, so our lives are passing and will soon end. Our lives are short and so time must be valued and used well. Similarly the motif of the scythe is a reminder of how all human life rises and is cut down. The Mason must understand and acknowledge that this is the final fate that we all share.

However, the brooding images of mortality and death are followed by the symbol of a sprig of acacia that reminds the Mason that, although our physical selves must die and be lost, our souls survive and live on. The image of the sprig of acacia comes from the Masonic story that it bloomed at the head of the grave of the murdered Master Mason Hiram Abiff.

# The Temple of Solomon

The biblical figure of King Solomon has always been said to have possessed great wisdom and, for Freemasons, he represents an archetypal leader or Grand Master who inspires reverence and offers an ideal role model. Solomon was the son of King David and Bathsheba. His mother assisted in Solomon becoming King after the death of his father in 961 BC. However, it is the story of the building of the Jewish Temple named after him that holds the greatest relevance for Freemasons. The Temple built by King Solomon is central to the iconography and traditions of modern Freemasonry. It is described in the Bible as being the first temple to be built by the Jewish people in Jerusalem. King David originally proposed the building of the temple and, during his lifetime, he had made preparations for its creation. As well as gathering workers for the project he drew up plans for its structure. It was intended to house the legendary Ark of the Covenant. The Ark was made from acacia wood and gold and held the pair of stone tablets, inscribed with the Ten Commandments, that Moses had been given by God. It also contained the rod of Aaron and a jar of manna. The lid of the Ark of the Covenant was called the mercy seat.

In *1 Chronicles 22* King David tells Solomon that he must build a Temple for the God of Israel and that he has provided him with 100,000 talents of gold, one million talents of silver and so much iron and bronze that it cannot be weighed. He also outlines how he has provided stone and timber for the building as well as masons, stonecutters and carpenters. In *1 Chronicles 28* King David gives Solomon not only instructions on the form that the Temple should take but detailed information about items that should be used within the building such as lamp stands, bowls and cups and the weight that they should be dependant on the material used such as gold and silver. King David reveals to his people that God had spoken to him and said that he could not build the Temple himself because he had been a warrior who had spilt blood. Instead God told him that he had chosen Solomon to build the Temple and that he would establish his kingdom forever if Solomon followed his commandments and kept the covenant that had been agreed with God. The Temple was to be built on Mount Moriah in Jerusalem where Abraham had offered his own son Isaac as a willing sacrifice to God.

Solomon decided to build a temple for the name of the Lord, and a royal palace for himself. Solomon conscripted 70,000 labourers and 80,000 stonecutters in the hill country, with 3600 to oversee them. Solomon sent word to King Hiram of Tyre:

Once you dealt with my father David and sent him cedar to build himself a house to live in. I am now about to build a house for the name of the Lord my God and dedicate it to him for offering fragrant incense before him, and for the regular offering of the rows of bread, and for burnt-offerings morning and evening, on the Sabbaths and the new moons and the appointed festivals of the Lord our God, as ordained for ever for Israel. The house that I am to build will be great, for our God is greater than other Gods... So now send me an artisan skilled to work in gold, silver, bronze and iron, and in purple, crimson and blue fabrics, trained also in engraving, to join the skilled workers who are with me in Judah and Jerusalem, whom my father David provided'. (*2 Chronicles 2: 1*)

## Hiram Abiff and Hiram King of Tyre

As we have seen, the unlawful murder of Hiram Abiff, architect and builder of the Temple of Solomon, is a dramatic story that is central to Masonic ritual. The building of the Temple of Solomon, as recorded in the Bible, actually mentions two individuals named Hiram. The first is Hiram King of Tyre whilst the second is a certain Hiram-abi who is described as a gifted master craftsman. It seems most likely that this is the Hiram described in Masonic lore. Hiram King of Tyre informs King Solomon that:

I have dispatched Hiram-abi, a skilled artisan, endowed with understanding, the son of one of the Danite women, his father a Tyrian. He is trained to work in gold, silver, bronze, iron, stone, and wood, and in purple, blue, and crimson fabrics and fine linen, and to do all sorts of engraving and execute any design that may be assigned him, with your artisans, the artisans of my lord, your father David... We will cut whatever timber you need from Lebanon, and bring it to you as rafts by sea to Joppa; you will take it up to Jerusalem... (*2 Chronicles 2: 13*)

In Freemasonry Hiram Abiff is often described as being 'the widow's son' and this epithet is based on the following passage from the bible.

Now King Solomon invited and received Hiram from Tyre. He was the son of a widow of the tribe of Naphtali, whose father, a man of Tyre, had been an artisan in bronze; he was full of skill, intelligence, and knowledge in working bronze. He came to King Solomon and did all his work. (*1 Kings 7: 13-14*)

Work is said to have commenced on building the Temple in the fourth year of King Solomon's reign on the second day of the second month. This puts the date at around 957 BC. The Bible itself does not provide much more information about Hiram the master craftsman and the story of his unlawful murder by Jubela, Jubelo and Jubelum as the temple was nearing completion belongs only to Masonic ritual and to legend. As we have already seen, King Solomon paid for the help of King Hiram with a form of tithe. In return for the cedar, cypress, manpower, skilled artisans and other materials for the building of the temple King Solomon provided food for the household of King Hiram. According to the Bible, he gave him a yearly supply of 20,000 cors of wheat and 20 cors of fine oil. During the building of the temple, Hiram produced furniture and adornments made from precious metals, including an important pair of pillars that were set at the entrance to the temple.

## Jachin and Boaz

The pillars cast by Hiram and set up at the vestibule of the temple have special symbolic significance within the iconography of Freemasonry. Their important symbolism and meaning is explained to candidates during the rituals of the First and Second Degrees:

> He cast two pillars of bronze. Eighteen cubits was the height of one, and a cord of twelve cubits would encircle it; the second pillar was the same... He set up the pillars at the vestibule of the temple; he set up the pillar on the south and called it Jachin; and he set up the pillar on the north and called it Boaz. (*1 Kings 7: 15-21*)

Boaz, the pillar that stood on the left of the porchway of the Temple of Solomon and which is recreated in modern Freemasonry lodges today, symbolises strength. Jachin stood as the right-hand pillar and symbolises wisdom and the act of establishment. When united they provide 'stability'. In Masonic images pillars are often shown surmounted by globes that represent the celestial and terrestrial spheres of existence.

As well as making the bronze pillars Jachin and Boaz, Hiram from Tyre, the son of the widow, created the 'sea of bronze'. This huge bowl-like receptacle was set on the backs of 12 bronze oxen with groups of three set at each corner of the compass. The giant bowl was around 4.5 metres in diameter, 2.4 metres in depth and was able to hold around 45,000 litres of water. The purpose of the 'sea of bronze', sometimes called the 'brazen sea' or 'molten sea', was to give the priests of the temple a means of purifying themselves through ritual immersion and cleansing of their bodies. Authors Christopher Knight and Robert Lomas, in their book *The Hiram Key*, have argued that the mysterious figure of Hiram Abiff is in fact based on the real-life Theban pharaoh Tao II the Brave.

As well as constructing the Temple itself, Solomon's builders made enormous efforts to provide the sacred site with fresh water which was essential to the rituals of purification that were held there. To this end huge underground cisterns were carved out of the stone upon which stood the citadel known as the Haram that defended the Temple itself. Water was conveyed to the cisterns by a specially constructed aqueduct called the 'aqueduct of Etam' because this was the origin of the flow of water. It has been estimated that one of the stone cisterns said to have been created by Solomon close to the temple was capable of storing 12 million litres of water. Appropriately enough, this underground chamber is referred to as the 'Great Sea'. Work continued on the great Temple of Solomon for seven years. According to Masonic legend it was at this point that Hiram Abiff, the Master Architect of the temple, was killed. After resolving the circumstances of his death, Solomon continued with the construction of the temple and appointed new trustworthy and loyal officers to carry out this work who were known as intendants of the building, a title that can still be found at higher levels of Masonic teaching. The temple was finally finished in 960 BC, the eleventh year of the reign of King Solomon.

When the new temple was complete, the Ark of the Covenant was brought from the tent temple called the Holy Tabernacle, where it had been kept, and was placed in the part of the building known as the Holy of Holies, the Kadosh Kadoshim. Before the Ark was put in place, King Solomon assembled all the people of Israel and they offered innumerable sacrifices of sheep and oxen to God. Once the Ark was placed inside, a cloud appeared in the temple and the building was filled with the glory of God. There followed a feast of dedication that lasted for seven days where prayers were said and sacrifices made marking a new chapter for the people of Israel and their relationship with God. The First Temple, as it is known, survived until 586 BC and its destruction at the hands of the Babylonians led by King Nebuchadnezzar. The Babylonians took the Hebrews into a captivity that lasted until they were finally set free when the Persian King Cyrus defeated the Babylonians in 538 BC.

The Hebrews returned to Jerusalem where plans were made for the erection of a new temple led by Zerubbabel. A second temple was begun on the site of the ruins of the first in 515 BC. When the Jewish leader Judah Maccabee took Jerusalem in 164 BC, he ordered that work be carried out on the Temple as it had fallen into a state of disrepair. King Herod also carried out work on the Temple until it was finally finished in 64 AD. However, this second temple was also destroyed in 70 AD, this time by the Romans. Today the only part of the Temple of Solomon that still stands is the famous Wailing Wall which remains a site of pilgrimage and veneration.

## Hermes Trismegistus

Two other figures from the ancient world whose influence looms large in the iconography and symbolism of Freemasonry are the man-god Hermes Trismegistus and the famous Greek philosopher and mathematician Pythagoras. It has been suggested that the roots of Freemasonry may lie in the culture of Ancient Egypt with its great traditions of temple building. Egyptian imagery and symbols are commonly found within the world of Freemasonry. The Egyptian God Hermes Trismegistus, meaning 'three times great Hermes' in Greek, is a figure who has appeared in Masonic legend and is equated with the Egyptian God Thoth. After Alexander the Great conquered Egypt a subsequent consequence of the Greek presence was the

Hellenisation of the native Gods. In Greek culture Hermes was the God of writing just as Thoth was in Egyptian culture. Their roles were combined in Hellenistic Greece in the form of Hermes Trismegistus who became a deity associated with astrology and magic. Both Gods also served the purpose of acting as guides to the souls of the dead. Hermes Trismegistus is said to be the bringer of wisdom who was the messenger of the Gods. He is also associated with trial and initiation and is credited with inventing writing and architecture, astronomy, geometry and other arts and sciences. Many of the ancient written sources of Egypt were said to have been produced by Hermes Trismegistus.

These written records formed a body referred to as the Hermetica or Hermetic literature and formed the magical education of Egyptian priests. These papyrus documents contained esoteric information about such subjects as rites of initiation within the Egyptian priesthood and the conjuring of spirits. It was believed that spirits could be trapped within statues and be made to perform a prophetic function by the priests, and Hermetic literature gave detailed information about how such magical feats could be achieved. It has been consistently stated by 'Hermeticists' that there are 42 works that can be attributed to Hermes Trismegistus. In some traditions, Hermes Trismegistus is seen as a real person who was the offspring of the great Hellenistic-Egyptian deity. The so-called Hermetic tradition was to have a dramatic impact on the development of alchemy, particularly in medieval Europe. However, it has been argued that the influence of the figure of Hermes Trismegistus also extended to the Islamic world where he is identified with Indris, the *nabi* of Surahs. He has also been identified with the biblical figure of Enoch in the Arabic world.

Hermeticism became popular in Western Europe after a body of texts known as the *Corpus Hermeticum* was brought to the Italian city of Pistoia in 1460. Pistoia was ruled by Cosimo de' Medici who had a particular interest in finding any written texts that had survived from the ancient world and used his position and influence to gather together such material. (Interestingly, Christian monasteries of the day proved to be repositories of esoteric and mystical lore.) The *Corpus* consisted of 16 books written in Greek that take the form of a number of dialogues between Hermes Trismegistus and other figures. The first book involves Hermes being taught by God about the mysteries of life and the universe and the majority of the following books feature Hermes passing on this secret, mystical knowledge to a number of others. Upon its rediscovery many believed that the *Corpus Hermeticum* was, in fact, a body of work older than the works of Plato. However, this contention was seriously challenged when a Swiss philologist called Isaac Casaubon examined the texts in 1614. Philology is the historical or comparative study of language and, when Casaubon scrutinised the *Corpus Hermeticum*, he concluded, on the basis of the style in which it was written, that it had actually been produced around the first few centuries following the birth of Christ. Subsequent historians have largely supported Casaubon's verdict on the approximate age of the texts.

Another text that has had a powerful impact on occult groups throughout history is the Emerald Tablet of Hermes Trismegistus. This work contains the philosophical idea that the pattern of the universe can be comprehended and understood through a realisation that all things are interlinked. This concept is the origin of the phrase 'As above, so below', that is widely known amongst many occult traditions. This can also be interpreted as meaning that individuals who gain an understanding of themselves can gain a greater understanding of existence.

One legend claims that Alexander the Great himself discovered the actual Emerald Tablet within the tomb of Hermes Trismegistus. The text of the Emerald Tablet of Hermes Trismegistus states that the wisdom of the whole universe is divided into three sections and that, because Hermes understood them all, he was known by his title of 'three times great'. The three areas of knowledge in which Hermes is said to have been versed are Astrology, Alchemy and Theurgy or supernatural magic. In the study of Astrology, Hermes looked beyond the physical aspects of the stars and planets to observe their symbolic meaning and the influence they cast on humanity. The primary goal of Alchemy is usually thought to be the transformation of base matter such as lead into gold. In Hermetic thought this is a metaphorical process that describes the transformation of an individual and the development of the soul. More specifically it can signify the growth and metamorphosis of an initiate into a Master whose potential is realised. Within the study of Theurgy Hermetic students learn practical skills in working supernatural magic with spirits such as the angels. Hermetic thought, it is argued, need not be restricted to any one particular religion and need not necessarily be viewed as constituting a religion in itself, a claim that is also made of Freemasonry. It is, therefore, a philosophical system for spiritual development that can be combined with religions such as Islam, Judaisim or Christianity. Nor need it embrace monotheistic religions only. It can even extend to pantheistic belief systems.

The Rosicrucian movement that began in mysterious circumstances in the seventeenth century, although it was based on Christianity, was influenced by Hermetic thought. It has been argued that the Rosicrucian movement had a significant impact on the development of Freemasonry. Within the structure of the Masonic Scottish Rite, the 18th degree is referred to as that of the Knight of the Rose Croix. The history and impact of Rosicrucianism on Freemasonry is discussed in further detail in Chapter Six.

## Pythagoras

Some authors and historians have argued that a link may exist between the famous Greek mathematician and philosopher Pythagoras and the roots of Freemasonry. Manly P Hall, for example, examines the influence of the teachings of Pythagoras on both Freemasonry and Rosicrucianism in his book *The Secret Teachings of All Ages*. Pythagoras was born on the Greek island of Samos, close to what is now the coastline of Turkey, in around 582 BC and founded his own secret religious and scientific society named the Pythagoreans. His father was called Mnesarchus and was a merchant from Tyre whilst his mother Pythais was born on Samos. He is best known for the mathematical theorem that bears his name which states that the square on the hypotenuse of a right-angled triangle is equal to the sum of the squares on the other two sides. Pythagoras left Samos when he was a youth and travelled to the city of Crotone in Southern Italy. He is said to have been advised by the philosopher Thales, who recognised his talents and ability, to travel to Memphis in Egypt to gain knowledge and training from the priests there who were renowned for their wisdom in the ancient world.

It is thought the academic school and secret society that Pythagoras formed in Crotone may have been based on the cult of Orpheus. Pythagoreans believed in the transmigration of the human soul and practiced rituals of purification similar to those found amongst the

Orphics. The Pythagoreans used the symbol of the five-pointed star known as the pentagram as an image that would be recognised by members of the group and as a motif of health and knowledge and it was used in initiation rites. It has been observed that the pentagram is a device used within Freemasonry during initiation ceremonies and can also be found as a design amongst the so-called 'jewels' or badges of office that Masters and Grand Masters of Masonry are entitled to wear. Pythagoras was particularly interested in music and Pythagoreans developed a numerical system that expressed the relationship of musical notes. The Pythagoreans believed that mathematical systems underpinned all things.

# Mystery Cults and Secret Societies

## The Cult of Dionysus

Masonic historians and other writers have drawn parallels between Freemasonry and many of the mystery cults and secret societies of the past. Whilst similarities can be observed between such groups and modern Masonry a clear link has never been categorically established. The cult of the Greek deity Dionysus, for example, is thought to have extremely ancient origins. The figure of Dionysus is, of course, most closely identified as the god of wine and intoxication and it is thought that his cult may have emerged in one form or another as early as 6000 BC with the first cultivation of wine during the Neolithic period. It has been speculated that his cult began in North Africa or in Asia Minor but it is generally held that the cult developed many of its most recognisable aspects in Minoan Crete. In ancient Greece, Dionysus was the god and patron of wine and winemaking but was also seen as a fertility figure linked with vegetation and wild animals. The first Mystery rituals probably took place on Crete in a period spanning 3000 BC to 1000 BC.

The cult of Dionysus involved a number of rites of initiation that marked different stages in the growth of an individual such as the transition to adulthood. Dionysus is also seen as the god of theatre and, in Athens, groups formed which held masked rituals enacting myths and legends linked to the god and which can be equated to the idea of a Masonic lodge.

The Great Dionysia was the major festival dedicated to Dionysus and was held in the Greek month of Elaphebolion. This was around the time of the Spring Equinox between March and April. It was held in Athens and the surrounding area during the classical period and took the form of a festival of theatre, drama and poetry. The inhabitants of Athens formed a procession and set out for the sanctuary of the god carrying symbolic phalluses as a recognition of Dionysus's role as a deity linked with fertility. The Great Dionysia is thought to have been preceded by an older festival that took place in rural areas known as the Lesser Dionysia that celebrated the production of the first wine. This took place around December and January and it was believed that, with the creation of this wine, Dionysus was symbolically re-born. Interestingly, Dionysus is also said to have converted water into wine and parallels between the cult of Dionysus and Christianity have been noted. It is thought that the Lesser Dionysia and other important festivals devoted to the god, such as the harvesting of the grapes, were times of ecstasy and abandonment and that they were times when initiation into the mystery cult of Dionysus would have taken place.

## The Eleusinian Mysteries

The Eleusinian Mysteries are amongst the earliest known Mystery Cults. They were based on the mythological story of Persephone and Demeter and important rituals of initiation were held in the Greek town of Eleusis, known today as Elefsina, which is not far from Athens. This ancient cult functioned as a secret society, revealing its ceremonies and beliefs only to the initiated.

It is thought that the Eleusinian Mysteries began around 1500 BC and the attendant ceremonies were performed every five years. This ancient Greek mystery cult also gained followers in Rome and its rituals were re-enacted over a period of around 2,000 years. They were open to a wide variety of people, including slaves, although anyone guilty of murder or 'barbarians', those who could not speak Greek, were excluded. Women could participate equally with men in the Eleusinian mysteries.

The central myth around which the mystery cult was based was that of the goddess of fertility and agriculture, Demeter, and her daughter Persephone. Demeter is one of the oldest of the Greek deities and was the daughter of Cronus and Rhea. She is particularly associated with crops such as wheat which, it was believed, she nurtured and protected. According to the ancient story, her daughter Persephone was seen by Hades (sometimes referred to as Pluto), the Lord of the dead and the Underworld, whilst she was with her friends the Oceanids. He was so enamoured of her beauty that he abducted her and carried her to the Underworld. She had been picking flowers and when she reached down to pick a particularly lovely narcissus the ground gave way and Hades dragged her down to the kingdom of the dead.

Although Persephone cried out loudly for her mother, Demeter was unable to find her and searched fruitlessly for nine days and nine nights. However, the sun god Helius had witnessed the abduction of Persephone and informed Demeter that Hades had taken her daughter. Persephone had been born of the union of Zeus with Demeter but her powerful father was not interested in her fate. So great was the sorrow of Demeter that she left Mount Olympus, home of the gods, and took the form of an unhappy old woman who searched the world for her missing daughter.

When Demeter arrived at Eleusis she sat down next to an olive tree by a well. As she sat next to the well the four daughters of King Celeus of Eleusis, whose names were Callidice, Demo, Clesidice and Callithoe, arrived to fetch water. When they saw how unhappy she was they asked her what was wrong. Demeter answered that she had been a prisoner of pirates and asked that they give her a job in their father's palace. On meeting the goddess disguised as an old woman, King Celeus agreed that she should become the nurse of his son Demophon. The goddess refused to eat or drink except when a female slave called Iambe made her laugh and managed to make her drink some barley-water.

Because of the kindness that the King and his wife Metaneira had shown, Demeter planned to show her thanks by making Demophon immortal. She rubbed ambrosia onto the young child's body and held him above a fire at night. However, one night Metaneira saw Demeter holding her child above the fire and, frightened that she was hurting her son, cried out. It was then that Demeter revealed her true identity and commanded King Celeus to build a temple for her at Eleusis, close to the well.

This, then, was said to be the beginning of the Eleusinian mysteries devoted to the goddess and her daughter. But, even after the temple had been built, Demeter continued to grieve and locked herself away in the new building away from people and the other gods. As a consequence, her misery and distress had a terrible effect upon the natural world as plants and trees died and the land was laid bare and wasted. As crops and harvests failed, the people began to starve. So serious was the situation that Zeus finally acted and sent Iris to Demeter to try to remedy the situation.

Iris failed and so Zeus told Hermes to visit Hades and request that he free Persephone. Hades agreed to the demands but, just as Persephone was leaving the subterranean underworld, he gave her six seeds of a pomegranate to eat. It was a trick. Because she had eaten the six seeds, she was now compelled to spend six months of the year with him in the underworld and the remaining six months with her mother. The months she spent with Demeter created Spring and Summer, when the natural world bloomed and was fertile in her presence, and the months she spent with Hades were bare as nature died away, creating Autumn and Winter. Whilst Persephone resided in the Underworld with Hades people would prepare for the new growth symbolised by the seeds she had eaten.

During the Eleusinian mysteries, the return of Persephone, symbolising the return of spring and new life, would be celebrated although the details of the rituals were kept secret. However, it is known that in the month of September, six months before the main ceremonies known as the Great Mysteries were conducted, a ritual called the Lesser Mysteries took place. The Lesser Mysteries were held beside the river Illisus that runs through Athens. The Greater Mysteries were staged at the sanctuary of Demeter below the Acropolis in Athens. Following the announcement that the Mysteries were underway, the next four days were devoted to offering sacrifices and rituals of purification held beside the sea. Once these rituals were completed a great procession of people would assemble and set out from Athens following a route known as the Sacred Way and travelled on to Eleusis.

The procession would halt at certain points, often

shrines, along the Sacred Way where further rituals took place. The procession was led by two key figures, the Hierophant and the Daduch. The Hierophant was said to reveal 'sacred things' to the initiates of the cult who were known as the 'mystes' whilst the Daduch known as the 'torch-bearer'. Apparently, when crossing the river Cephissus, the mystes would share jokes with one another and this part of the procession focussed on laughter and jubilant behaviour. The congregation would reach Eleusis late that evening and the main ceremony of the Mysteries took place the day after.

It is said that the worshippers offered sacrifices to Demeter and Persephone but that they went without eating in imitation of Demeter when she was searching for her daughter. Like the goddess, they too would drink only some barley water. Some historians have argued that the drink of barley water known as 'kykeon' was mixed with pennyroyal and that the mixture had a hallucinogenic effect on the participants. The authors R Gordon Wasson, Carl AP Buck and Albert Hoffman suggested in their book *The Road to Eleusis*, that the importance and longevity of the Mysteries stemmed from a powerful psychoactive element in the kykeon. It has been hypothesised that it may have been created by the presence of a fungus called ergot that can be a parasite on barley and is capable of producing a similar effect in people to that of LSD or 'magic mushrooms'.

The main rituals, about which very little is known, would have taken place within the temple devoted to

Demeter and Persephone. They would have entered a great hall within the temple called the Telesterium, which translates as 'hall of rituals'. Interestingly, although the exact nature of what went on during the ceremonies is not known, it is widely believed that they were held at night and the events were probably illuminated by torches. The rituals were divided into three main sections: firstly, the 'legomena', or 'that which was said', perhaps involving a retelling of the Persephone myth; secondly, the 'dromena', 'that which was done', that may have involved some form of ritual drama; and finally the 'deiknyomena', 'that which was shown'. In the final part of the ceremony, the deiknyomena, the hierophant would enter the most sacred part of the temple, the anactorum or 'the palace', where he would show the initiates relics sacred to the goddess Demeter. Initiates swore never to reveal what they had seen under penalty of death. Through the course of the ceremony, the initiates attained a state known as 'epopteia', a state of purity, and also perhaps, through fasting and chemical means, achieved a belief in the potential for rebirth.

Although the Eleusinian Mysteries gained great popularity in Greece and in the Roman world, they declined in importance with the ascension of Christianity. The sanctuaries sacred to the Hellenistic gods were banned from performing their rituals under the Roman Emperor Theodosius I who issued a decree to that effect in 392 AD. It has been observed that there are similarities between the Eleusinian Mysteries and Freemasonry.

There are parallels to be found in the insistence on secrecy and in a hierarchical system of initiates who are threatened with death for revealing the inner mysteries of their order. Similarly, both the Eleusinian Mysteries and Freemasonry hold their ceremonies in temples clearly divided in terms of symbolic importance and meaning. They also both have as their aim the development and growth of the individual through a series of revelatory rituals in which the candidate achieves a higher state of self-knowledge.

## Gnostic Gospels

The authors Christopher Knight and Robert Lomas, in their speculative study of the origins of Freemasonry *The Hiram Key*, have argued that Gnostic thought may have played an important part in its development. The term Gnostic is usually applied to a body of early Christian writings that diverge from the teachings of the New Testament, as it is understood today. The word comes from the Greek 'gnosis' meaning 'knowledge' or 'understanding' and, in this context, it relates to spiritual, secret or inner knowledge that can illuminate a path to God. The discovery of the preserved early Christian manuscripts called the Dead Sea Scrolls, along with the Gnostic Gospels found at Nag Hammadi in Upper Egypt, has caused considerable debate about the 'true' nature of Christianity in recent years.

In December 1945, an Arab boy accidentally stumbled upon the Gnostic Gospels, contained in a sealed jar that had been buried in the ground close to the Egyptian town of Nag Hammadi. The jar contained 52 scrolls made from papyrus and written in Coptic. They are thought to date from around 350 to 400 AD. Although it must be remembered that they do not necessarily represent a single overall coherent religious viewpoint, they are notable for offering a radically different interpretation of the death and resurrection of Jesus Christ. Knight and Lomas point particularly to the Gnostic theme of an individual obtaining resurrection whilst alive. In this interpretation, the living are effectively spiritually dead until they undergo some form of spiritual awakening and are therefore viewed as having been resurrected. Knight and Lomas quote from the Gnostic Gospel of Philip that makes this point, saying, 'those who say they will die first and then rise are in error, they must receive the resurrection while they live'. (Christopher Knight and Robert Lomas, *The Hiram Key*, p.50)

For Knight and Lomas, the concept of achieving a living resurrection can also be found within the Masonic ceremony of the Third Degree and they have speculated that a link might exist between Gnostic thought and Freemasonry. They also observed striking parallels between the ritual of becoming a Mark Mason and concepts found within the Gospel of Thomas in which Jesus says, 'Show me the stone which the builders have rejected. That one is the cornerstone.' The Gospel of

Matthew, Mark and Luke record differing versions of the same event but the Gospel of Thomas resembles most closely the ritual carried out during the Masonic Mark Masonry degree. They also argued that the Gospel of Matthew points to a hidden tradition of the teachings of Christ when Jesus tells the disciples that only they have been instructed in the 'mysteries of heaven'.

## Mithraism

Many have observed clear parallels between what is known of the ancient mystery religion of Mithraism and Freemasonry and, for some, these hint at a possible link between the two. The worship of the god Mithras in one form or another is thought to date back as much as 3,500 years and it spanned cultures as far apart as India and Roman Britain. The cult of Mithras became particularly prevalent in the Western Roman Empire from about 67 BC until its fall several centuries later. It has been argued that early Christianity and the cult of Mithras had a surprisingly large number of features in common and that, if Roman culture had not embraced Christianity, it could have become Mithrasian.

Both religions feature saviour gods born on 25 December who offer salvation through faith, knowledge and compassion. Mithraism was particularly popular amongst the Roman military but was also open to the poor and to slaves and, like Christianity, involved a sacrament in which wine served to symbolise sacrificial blood. During a ceremonial meal, small loaves of bread marked with a cross were eaten and they symbolised sacrificial flesh. Mithrasians referred to one another as 'brothers' and were ministered to by a leader called 'father'. Interestingly, the symbols of his station were a hat modelled on the hat of Phrygian origin worn by Mithras himself in many depictions of the god, a staff, a ring and a hooked sword. D Jason Cooper, amongst others, has argued that Christianity adopted these aspects of Mithraism. It turned the staff and sword into the shepherd's crook and made the floppy Phrygian cap stand upright and, by naming the resulting headgear a 'mitre', even acknowledged its origins in the cult of Mithras. As well as influencing the attire of bishops, Mithraism also featured a 'father of fathers' who, much like the pope, resided in Rome and administered to the needs of the believers. Although little is known about the theological structure and beliefs of Mithraism, it has been speculated, on the basis of written sources and surviving archaeological material in the form of temples, statues and reliefs carved in stone, that its initiates passed through seven degrees or stages of development.

Both Mithraism and Freemasonry, then, feature the concept of its members passing through stages of development. They have also both served as secret societies in which special knowledge is limited to certain key individuals within the group. Both were groups fundamentally aimed at men. Many of those who joined the cult of

Mithras were drawn from the upper echelons of Roman culture such as the Emperors Commodus and Trajan. Freemasonry in Britain has exhibited a similar tendency to recruit its members from the aristocracy and nobility. Interestingly, it has been conjectured that, whilst Roman men worshipped Mithras, their wives may have been part of women-only religions such as the cult of Cybele. Cooper has also pointed out that Freemasonry and Mithraism 'represent stages in a wider continuum of religion' (D Jason Cooper, *Mithras: Mysteries and Initiations Rediscovered*, p. 35).

Mithraism was compatible with the old religions of Rome and Greece because it incorporated them into its world-view. Freemasonry does not claim to be a religion in itself and embraces a wide variety of faiths, seeing its purpose as the spiritual development of the individual within their own personal cultural beliefs. It is therefore able to be of relevance to any number of different religions. Both Mithraism and Freemasonry have also stressed the importance of high moral standards in its members, although it is, of course, possible that Mithraism may also have acted (as some claim Freemasonry has done) as something of 'an old boys' network'. However, unlike Freemasonry, the cult of Mithras had an established class of priests who administered to the needs of its members.

## Druids

The common claim that Freemasonry has ancient origins has, perhaps unsurprisingly, led some to conjecture that it may be linked to the Druids of the Celtic world. The Druids were the powerful priests of what are broadly termed Celtic cultures and the description 'Celtic' can generally be said to apply to large expanses of Western Europe during the Iron Age. The term 'Celt' derives from the Greek word 'Keltoi' which was something of a blanket description to denote those tribes that inhabited the lands to the west of the river Rhine. What is known of the Druids has survived largely due to reports by contemporary Roman writers whose expanding empire superseded the existing power structures of which the Druidic class formed an important part. Druidic lore was said to have been committed to memory, as the societies in which Druidry was found were primarily oral cultures. Julius Caesar observed that the Gauls and Britons only used writing to record such information as accounts. He records that they used Greek to this effect, although it is likely that, at the time he was writing, Latin was used for this purpose as well.

The British Isles were considered to be a particularly important centre for the Druids and potential candidates for education in its practices were sent there from ancient Gaul. It is said that Druids underwent extended periods of training in learning and memorising Druidic lore, training that could last up to 20 years. There were a number of important centres or schools for Druids in Britain including Anglesey, the Isle of Man and a number of the Scottish Islands. The importance of the Druids within their societies is perhaps best demonstrated by the fact that they did not have to pay taxes like ordinary people and were also not compelled to give any form of military service. However, their role was more than simply religious. Within Celtic culture, they also acted as judges and arbiters in disputes at both the personal and individual level and between different tribes or clans.

What is known of their religious beliefs is that they venerated a number of different gods and goddesses but also saw many elements of the natural world as sacred. According to Roman writers like Pliny, they held their rituals in sacred oak groves and there is some evidence to suggest that they may have offered human sacrifices to their Gods. The Roman writers who reported the lurid details of such events generally adopt a tone of shock and horror which is surely ironic when Roman culture itself could happily incorporate practices such as widespread crucifixion or the bloody excesses of the Coliseum. The Druids were often called upon to divine the future and act as seers within their cultures but it is likely that, Roman propaganda aside, they were learned and educated individuals with knowledge of science, the arts, astronomy, philosophy and medicine.

Julius Caesar wrote that the belief that was central to their worldview was that, when an individual dies, the body may be lost but the human soul carries on and is effectively reincarnated in another body through metempsychosis. The secretive nature of Druidic rituals and customs, the memorising of arcane law and their powerful position within their respective societies, and the belief that physical death is followed by rebirth have all been linked with the world of Freemasonry. If a genuine link exists between the two it is unknown but it is worth remembering that interest in the Druids was revived in the seventeenth and eighteenth centuries and it seems likely that ideas from the ancient past may have influenced the development of Freemasonry in this period.

## Essenes

A controversial and much disputed contention is that Freemasonry can trace its origins to the ancient Jewish sect known as the Essenes. This religious movement was in existence between the second century BC and the first century AD. Most of what is known of the Essenes and their beliefs comes from the accounts of a Jewish historian called Josephus who lived in the first century AD. Josephus relates that, at the time he was writing, there were three main important Jewish sects. They were the Essenes, the Sadducees and the Pharisees. Many have argued that members of the Essene community were the authors of the Dead Sea Scrolls which were found in caves near Qumran in 1947. However, the term Essene is thought likely to apply to a number of Jewish groups who shared similar ideas and practices but which also held divergent ideas on points of religious beliefs and practices.

The authors Christopher Knight and Robert Lomas, in their book *The Hiram Key*, argue that there are numerous similarities between Masonic practices and what is known of the Essenes. Unlike the Sadducees and the Pharisees, whose members were born into their communities, the Essene community, like modern Freemasonry, created its membership through individual invitations to join. Knight and Lomas also note that the Essene community, based, in their opinion, at Qumran, was extremely hierarchical, with a 'Guardian' or 'Grand Master' at its head.

They also point to the fact that the Essene community had different stages or levels of membership and that entry to these required candidates or novices to take vows of secrecy. Breaching these promises in the Essene community could carry terrible punishments. Masonic candidates who take vows to join the Order are also warned that horrible punishments await them if they break their promises, although these are understood to be symbolic not actual. Knight and Lomas also point to the Essene habit of wearing white robes to demonstrate their purity and their claim that they possessed some form of secret knowledge.

## Medieval Stonemasons

Many have argued that Freemasonry developed from stonemasons of the medieval period. They were sometimes referred to as 'freemasons'. This may derive from the fact that these men were free to move from one work site to another, enjoying an independence of travel and employment, and were not the serfs of any particular lord. It may derive from the French term 'franc macon' meaning a man who works in a lodge in the employment of the Church and was exempt from taxes levied on other tradesmen. Another explanation is that it identifies the type of stone that they were particularly skilled at working, being 'free stone' a softer chalk-based material. Those who worked in harder material were called 'hard hewers' or 'rough masons'. The 'free stone masons' were recognised as being more highly skilled craftsmen who were able to perform detailed and finely rendered work in the softer stone.

The earliest known Masonic text to survive to the present day is known as the Halliwell manuscript or the Regius poem. It was 'discovered' during the 1830s in the King's Library of the British Museum. It was subsequently published by James O. Halliwell in 1840. The manuscript poem is made up of 64 pages or 794 lines of poetic verse. Estimates as to its age have varied. A strong consensus of opinion puts its earliest possible date as around 1390 but some believe it was produced as late as 1445. Its Latin title is *Hic incipint constitutiones artis gemetrioe secundum Euclydum* which translates as 'Here begin the constitutions of geometry according to Euclid'. Its opening section describes a legend that Masonry was founded in Egypt by the celebrated mathematician Euclid and goes on to state that Freemasonry was introduced to Britain during the reign of King Athelstan. This English king reigned from 924 AD to 939 AD. The poem relates how Prince Edwin was an early patron of the Craft and is said to have presided over an assembly of Masons. The document also lays out 15 articles and 15 points as to how the society should be governed and provides guidelines for assemblies of Masons.

# The Knights Templar

Perhaps the most popular and persistent theory about the origins of Freemasonry is that it has it roots in the crusades of the Middle Ages and began with the military order of warrior monks known as the Knights Templar. This idea was put forward as early as 1737 in a lecture in Paris by Andrew Michael Ramsay. The Ramsay Oration, as many Masons termed it, proved to be very controversial and divided opinion as to its credibility. In more recent years many writers have attempted to link the Knights Templar with the foundation and development of Freemasonry, perhaps most notably Christopher Knight and Robert Lomas in *The Hiram Key*. They have argued that many parallels can be observed between modern Masonic practices and what is known about the legendary order of crusaders. Supposed historical events surrounding the building of the Temple of Solomon are central to Masonic rituals. The knights took their name from that Temple because King Baldwin II, the Patriarch of Jerusalem, had granted them living quarters on the site where it had been. Knight and Lomas argue that secret knowledge, passed down through history by a number of different groups, was discovered by the Templars on the site of the Temple.

They also point to the practice of Templar clerics wearing white gloves whilst they were consecrating the bread and wine of the Eucharist and the fact that modern day Freemasons also wear white gloves at Lodge meetings. They also note that Templars would wear tight sheepskin breeches under their outer clothing as a symbol of their chastity and innocence. They draw parallels between these items of clothing and the white lambskin aprons worn by Freemasons which are said to symbolise innocence and friendship. They also observe that the battle flag of the Knights Templar, known as the Beausant, could be linked with Masonic symbolism in the modern era. The battle flag was divided into two vertical blocks, one in black and the other in white. For the Templars, the black section of their flag symbolised the profane world of sin from which they had turned in order to commit themselves to the Templar order, represented by the white section of the flag. In modern Masonic ritual candidates are said to move from a state of darkness towards the light of initiation into the Brotherhood. Modern lodges also have a patterned floor made of black and white squares and Masons are expected to attend meetings wearing black suits and ties with white shirts. If they do not do so, they are thought to be improperly attired and barred from attending.

## The Founding of the Order

The military order of the Knights Templar was founded in about 1119 in the holy city of Jerusalem. Upon their inception they were known as the Order of Poor Knights of the Temple of Solomon, a title generally abbreviated to the Knights Templar. Their stated purpose was to protect pilgrims travelling on the road to Jerusalem following the Christian success of the First Crusade. Their founders were the French knights Hugues de Payen from Champagne and Godfrey de St Omer from Picardy who had both fought in the First Crusade.

Although the Christians had taken the major cities of the Holy Land, the roads were dangerous for the growing numbers of pilgrims to travel and groups were regularly attacked en route to the sacred sites they hoped to visit. On one occasion during the Easter of 1119 a large group of 700 pilgrims was ambushed by a Saracen force who managed to kill 300 of them and to capture a further 60 for sale as slaves. When the Order was first formed, it consisted of nine knights and, according to some sources, it remained at that number until 1127 when Hugues de Payen travelled to France to recruit new members and to have the Order officially recognised. The Knights Templar were an innovation for their time in that they functioned both as a military force and a monastic order.

During their existence as a military order, they developed great power and influence throughout Europe.

Their numbers rapidly swelled and they gained donations of property, land and money to assist in their
efforts in the Holy Land or Outremer, 'the land beyond
the seas', as it was referred to in the medieval West.
Together with the Knights Hospitaller, on whom they
were partly based, they became the most significant
military order of the crusades. As an order of monks,
they were provided with a 'rule' or code of conduct by
St Bernard of Clairvaux. This was based on the rule of
the Cistercians, the monastic order to which Bernard
himself belonged. Furthermore, the Templars were
answerable to no authority other that that of the Pope
himself, a condition granted them to provide the
freedom to pursue their goal of safeguarding pilgrims
and protecting Christian interests in Outremer.

The popular image of a Templar is a knight on horse-
back, wearing white with a distinctive red cross, but the
order was, in fact, divided into four distinctive groups.
These included chaplains, who served as priests, and
brothers who maintained and ran the holdings of the
Templars or performed trade work to support the
order. The Knights themselves acted as heavy cavalry
and, as part of their rule, were granted permission to
wear white habits whilst the sergeants served as light
cavalry and wore brown habits. Knights were recruited
from powerful and noble families and the sergeants were
drawn from more humble backgrounds. The Templars
went on to serve not only in the Holy Land, fighting
against the Saracens, but also in other religious conflicts

between Christians and Muslims in Portugal and Spain.

In many ways, the Templars were like one of today's international corporations. They had properties and holdings throughout Europe, they were involved in manufacture and trade and they also developed a system of banking that was extremely innovative. Pilgrims travelling to the Holy Land were able to leave possessions or money at one of the Temple preceptories or properties and gain letters of credit that could be reimbursed on arrival.

## Charges of Heresy

In 1307, the Grand Master of the Knights Templar Jacques de Molay travelled to France to meet with Pope Clement V. The Grand Master was summoned by the Pope to discuss the possible merging of the Templars and the other great military order of the day, the Knights Hospitaller. Discussions were also to be held on a new crusade. Whilst these issues were being debated Jacques de Molay also requested that the Pope look into allegations made against several Templars of gross impropriety that had led to their expulsion from the Order in 1305.

The incident had damaged the image of the Order and Jacques de Molay hoped to clear its name. Clement wrote to Philip IV, 'the Fair', King of France, to inform him that he planned reluctantly to investigate the Order. Philip had not been given any orders to proceed further but, on Friday 13 October 1307, he had all Templars in

France arrested and charged with blasphemy, sodomy and heresy. (According to popular legend, the origin of the idea that Friday the 13th is an unlucky day stems from the arrest of the Templars on this date.) However, the real motivation for Philip's actions is thought to have been a desire to take for himself the wealth and property that the Templars had accrued. Philip, who had a history of debt and insolvency, persecuted other groups within French society, including the Jews and the Lombards, and similarly seized their wealth.

When, in 1301, Pope Boniface VIII had published a papal bull, Unam Sanctum, that had aimed to assert the authority of Rome over all other authorities and had prepared to excommunicate the French King for infringing that authority, Philip had responded by having him arrested on charges of murder, heresy and sodomy. Only the intervention of the people of Agnani, where the Pope was being held captive, had saved Boniface, forcing the French force sent by Philip to leave the city and allowing the Pope to escape to Rome. However, the shock of the ordeal appears to have led directly to his death a mere four weeks later. The French King had put considerable pressure on the new Pope, Clement, to condemn the Order but, initially at least, Clement was reluctant to do so and, in fact, had castigated Philip for his actions. He had quickly sent Philip an angry letter stating that:

> You, our dear son... have, in our absence, violated every rule and laid hands on the persons and properties of the

Templars. You have also imprisoned them and, what pains us even more, you have not treated them with due leniency... Your hasty act is seen by all, and rightly so, as an act of contempt towards ourselves and the Roman Church. (quoted in Piers Paul Read, *The Templars*, p.265)

Now it rapidly emerged that the King was determined to proceed with his action against the Templars and effectively bullied and intimidated Clement into supporting him. Through vicious torture, mass confessions of guilt were extracted from the Templars in France, including the Grand Master Jacques de Molay who had been arrested near Paris by Philip's particularly cruel henchman William de Nogaret. It was claimed by their inquisitors that the Order worshipped the devil and that every new recruit was informed upon joining the Templars that Jesus Christ was a false prophet. His crucifixion had not been the salvation of the world but he had been simply a man who was punished in this way for his sins. Templars admitted to trampling the cross during their ritual of admission to the Order and also to performing obscene kisses upon one another during the ceremony.

Particular attention was paid to the confession that Templars had worshipped a false idol called Baphomet. The form that Baphomet took varied from confession to confession. Sometimes it appeared as a cat but, most commonly, it was said to be a head of some description. As a symbol of their veneration of their idol, the

Templars were said to wear cords around their waists that had brushed or touched Baphomet. As a sign of their rejection of Jesus Christ as the Son of God, it was claimed by their prosecutors that the priests of the Templars would leave out the words of consecration whilst performing Mass. Other confessions extracted under torture played upon prejudices that were held against the Order, that they were greedy and material-istic and that their aim was to accrue great wealth for themselves. The Templars, who had often been blamed for the loss of the Holy Land, were even said to have been in league with Muslim forces.

## Trial of the Templars

The charges made against the Order had been met with consternation outside France but, faced by what appeared to be general admissions of guilt from the majority of Templars questioned, including Jacques de Molay, Pope Clement ordered the widespread arrest of its members and seizure of its property. It is thought that the Pope was attempting to regain some control over the outcome of the situation. Encouraged by Clement's involvement, Jacques de Molay, when he met with three cardinals whom the Pope had sent to question him, retracted the confession that he had given. He is said to have told them that his confession was only made whilst under torture. Following the Grand Master's recanting of his confession, others within the Order followed suit.

However, those who undertook this course of action in the hope that the Pope would treat them fairly and leniently were also putting themselves in a very dangerous position. According to the rules of the Inquisition all relapsed heretics (which is what the Templars had technically become) were bound to be placed under the jurisdiction of secular law and would be sentenced to be burnt to death.

When the Pope refused to condemn the Templars, the French King threatened to make the same charges against him that had been brought to bear on the Order. But Pope Clement initially stood firm on the matter. In June 1308, Clement travelled to Poitiers to hear the confessions of 72 Templars sent by Philip and, under pressure, the Pope agreed to open further enquiries into the Order. Legal complications in the case of the Templars meant that the swift action Philip had intended against them was frustrated. However, in June 1308, he simply returned to the impulsive actions for which he had become known and had 58 members of the Order burnt to death as relapsed heretics, a number that included two Templars who had been defending their case in court. Finally, in 1311, Clement issued a papal bull that dissolved the Order and stated that the property of the Templars should be handed over to the Hospitallers.

In 1313, the final fate of the Grand Master Jacques de Molay and three other important figures within the Order was decided by the Pope. They were declared to be heretics outside the cathedral of Notre Dame in Paris and sentenced to spend the rest of their lives in jail. At this moment Jacques De Molay, who was now around the age of 70 and had suffered years of imprisonment, declared that the Templars were innocent of the charges made against them and was supported by the Preceptor of Normandy, Geoffroi de Charney, who also recanted his confession. But Philip moved swiftly against the senior Templars in order to deny the Order any possibility of clearing its name. As relapsed heretics, Jacques de Molay and Geoffroi de Charney were ordered to be burnt to death at the stake. At around the hour of vespers, they were taken out on to a small island in the river Seine called the Ile-des-Javiaux. It is said that Jacques de Molay once again protested the innocence of the Order and declared that Pope Clement and the French King Philip the Fair would be summoned to appear before God before the year had ended. In the event Jacques de Molay was burned at the stake but his final wish was granted. Both the Pope and the king died within 12 months.

## Rosslyn Chapel

It is thought that the Templars may have had some fore-warning of what Philip was planning against them. The fabled treasure that the Templars were said to possess was never found and it has been claimed that important relics and/or documents were smuggled out of the Paris preceptory prior to the arrests of 13 October 1307. One of the great unanswered questions about the Order is what fate befell the fleet of ships belonging to the Templars that was based at the French port of La Rochelle. It has been suggested that the Templar treasure, whatever it may have been, was taken to La Rochelle from where an unrecorded number of ships left France. It is known that the fleet disappeared mysteriously but the final destination of the ships is unknown. Michael Baigent and Richard Leigh have argued the case that a group of Templars fled persecution in France and headed north by sea to Scotland. They speculate that, in Scotland, the Templars found an ally in Robert the Bruce who had himself been excommunicated by the Pope and that they went on to aid him in his victory at the Battle of Bannockburn. In their book *The Temple and the Lodge* Baigent and Leigh make the suggestion that the Templars found a permanent sanctuary in Scotland and that it was their influence that resulted in the development of Scottish Freemasonry.

Many have argued that the architecture of the remarkable Rosslyn Chapel points to the influence and presence of the Knights Templar in Scotland. Rosslyn Chapel is located in the village of Roslin in Midlothian and was founded as the Collegiate Chapel of St Matthew by William Sinclair. Sinclair was the First Earl of Caithness and a member of an important Scottish family which was to develop strong connections with Scottish Freemasonry. The first Grand Master of the Grand

Lodge of Scotland was also called William Sinclair and was a descendant of the man who founded Rosslyn Chapel in 1446. A number of other Sinclairs also held the post of Grand Master at later dates. The Sinclair family name is sometimes also spelt as 'St Clair'.

The design and decoration of the building has been the source of considerable speculation and conjecture and some authors find hidden meaning and significance within the fabric of the building itself. The chapel contains many examples of carvings of the 'Green Man'. These carvings depict a human face surrounded by foliage and vegetation, usually with leaves issuing from its mouth. They are generally viewed as fertility figures and are widely accepted as being pre-Christian images. Authors Christopher Knight and Robert Lomas, amongst others, have suggested that the chapel contains carvings of the aloe cactus and maize cobs. According to accepted history, at the time that the Chapel was built such plants were not known within Europe because America had not yet been discovered. It has been suggested that this provides evidence that members of the Sinclair family, connected to the Knights Templar, had actually travelled to America and brought back such knowledge before Christopher Columbus. More prosaically, the carvings in question have also been interpreted as depictions of lilies or wheat. On the basis of archaeological digs carried out in the nineteenth century, some scholars have thought that Rosslyn Chapel was actually originally intended to be a much larger building. Christopher Knight and Robert Lomas put forward the hypothesis that the west wall of the chapel was actually intended to represent the Wailing Wall, the surviving part of the Temple of Solomon in Jerusalem.

Interest has also focussed on three pillars within the chapel, which are known as the Master Pillar, the Journeyman Pillar and the Apprentice Pillar. They stand at the east end of the chapel and are the subject of a local legend. It is said that a mason working in the chapel left his apprentice to carve its elaborate surface but did not think he was skilled enough to perform the work. However, when the apprentice completed the carving, the mason became so angry and jealous of this remarkable feat that he killed him by striking him a cruel and fatal blow to the head with a wooden mallet.

## Priory of Sion

Probably the most infamous and controversial theory about the Knights Templar to be aired in recent times links the medieval military order to a supposed Masonic-style secret society known as the Priory of Sion. Most obviously, this highly contentious hypothesis formed the basis for the best-selling *The Holy Blood and the Holy Grail* by Michael Baigent, Richard Leigh and Henry Lincoln and that led in turn to *The Da Vinci Code* by Dan Brown. Both books argue that the purpose for the existence of the alleged Priory of Sion was to guard and protect an ancient secret concerning the real nature of the mythical Holy Grail.

They argue that a secret order, most commonly referred to as 'Prieuré de Sion' or the Priory of Sion, created the Knights Templar as its administrative and military arm to protect a previously unknown secret that the bloodline of Jesus Christ has survived throughout history. It is also claimed that this secret knowledge was known to the many prominent figures who served as Grand Master or 'Nautonnier' of the Order. Nautonnier is an old French word that translates as navigator or helmsman. Some of the individuals who are alleged to have been past Grand Masters of the Order include such famous real-life figures as the artist Leonardo da Vinci, the scientist and mathematician Sir Isaac Newton, the celebrated author Victor Hugo, classical composer Claude Debussy and the poet and artist Jean Cocteau.

It is often claimed that the Knights Templar, whose stated aim was to protect pilgrims travelling to the Holy Land, were actually involved in carrying out excavations of some kind beneath the Temple Mount in Jerusalem. The Templars did carry out building work there and there does seem to be some evidence that they had carried out excavations beneath the platform of the Temple Mount where legends claimed numerous holy relics had been deposited. When the Royal Engineers were carrying out surveying work beneath the Temple Mount in 1894, a number of Templar relics were discovered, indicating their presence there at some point. It is said that the Order had been digging in the area known as Solomon's Stables and there has been considerable conjecture over what they were looking for and what, if anything, they found.

Authors Christopher Knight and Robert Lomas, amongst others, have conjectured that the Templars may have found a hidden collection of early Gnostic Christian writings, preserved as scrolls or tablets, and that these influenced their beliefs and led to the charges of heresy made against them. Other suggestions about the nature of the supposed Templar discovery have included the Ark of the Covenant or the Holy Grail, the exact nature of which, as we have seen, has been the cause of great speculation.

However, it is now accepted that the Priory of Sion was in fact a deception that has an equally bizarre story related to it. The Priory was an association that was founded in 1956 by Pierre Plantard, Jean Delaval, André Bonhomme and Armand Defago. Plantard was at the centre of the Priory of Sion, which can be viewed variously as a surrealist joke, a hoax or a confidence trick. Plantard, in particular, believed that he was a serious claimant to the throne of France and used the group in an attempt to further his ambitions. In order to 'prove' that the Priory of Sion had originated during the medieval period, Plantard produced a series of fake documents that were placed in the Bibliothèque Nationale in Paris. He also created a story that, in 1891, a priest called Father Berenger Saunière from Rennes-Le-Chateau in the south of France had discovered these documents in his church. Plantard then promoted this story, which appeared to validate the authenticity of the Priory of Sion, by working with a French author called Gérard de Sède. The resulting book was published in 1967 and was called *Le Trésor Maudit de Rennes-le-Chateau*, which translates as the 'Accursed Treasure of Rennes-le-Chateau'. The book featured Plantard's fake documents and claimed that the priest had become rich after making some kind of mysterious discovery. When police searched Plantard's house in 1993 they unearthed a collection of false papers that he had produced in an attempt to validate his claims to royal status. He later went on to admit that the Priory of Sion had been a complete hoax and that he had invented everything largely to live out his personal dreams and fantasies.

# The Development of Freemasonry in Europe

The development of Freemasonry appears to have had two main phases. The first phase was the establishment of the craft guilds of operative stonemasons who appear to have had comparatively simple rituals associated with their organisations. The second phase in the development of Freemasonry is the move towards speculative Masonry where individuals from outside the profession of stonemasonry begin to be admitted to the lodges.

As we have seen, the Regius Poem or Halliwell document dating from around 1390 is the oldest known Masonic document. The second oldest known document that relates to Masonry is the Cooke manuscript that dates to around 1450 and is named after Matthew Cooke who edited it for publication in 1861. The Cooke manuscript, unlike the Regius poem, contains information of a speculative nature and is thought to have been written by a Mason. However, knowledge of the development and growth of Freemasonry from this period until the late sixteenth and the seventeenth centuries is sparse. In 1425, it is recorded that a decree was issued on behalf of King Henry VI (who was only three at the time) that

English Masons were forbidden to hold assemblies. It had apparently been noted that the working lodges had developed links that unified them.

The Schaw Statutes dating from 1598 and 1599 give a fuller picture of Masonic practices in Scotland at this time. They are named after William Schaw who was the Master of Works and Warden General for King James VI of Scotland and detail the duties of lodge members. They also ban lodge members from undertaking work with unqualified Masons. The statutes reveal that Masons who produced poor work of a low standard could expect certain penalties as punishment. They also allude to Masons sharing knowledge of a spiritual nature.

Interestingly, the statutes also require that the lodges should test their member's abilities in memorising information. Information about lodges begins to grow around this time in Scotland because these statutes require lodges to keep written records. The Minutes of the Aitchison's Haven Lodge and St Mary's Lodge, based in Edinburgh, have survived from 1599. It is recorded that Laird Boswell of Auchenleck was initiated into a Scottish Lodge in 1600. Because Lord Boswell was not an operative Mason, he is regarded as being amongst the earliest known speculative Masons. In England very little documentary material has survived from before 1717. From this period onwards Freemasonry underwent a growing process of gentrification.

## The Renaissance

One of the earliest written records of a Freemason being admitted to a lodge in England can be found in the diary of the noted antiquary Elias Ashmole. On 16 October 1646, Ashmole wrote that, 'I was made a Free Mason at Warrington, in Lancashire, with Henry Mainwaring, of Karincham, in Cheshire.' Born on 23 May 1617 in Lichfield, Ashmole had a colourful life, combining an involvement with the politics of the day with a keen interest in alchemy and astrology. A royalist, Ashmole supported Charles I during the English Civil War. His major passion was acquiring unusual and varied artefacts. He combined his own collections with that of the botanist John Tradescant the younger and donated the material to Oxford University in 1677. A specially commissioned building was designed by Sir Christopher Wren to house the collection and finished in 1682 and named the Ashmolean Museum in honour of its donor. He appears to have maintained an active involvement with Freemasonry throughout his life, recording in his diary entry of 10 March 1682 that he had attended a lodge meeting at Masons' Hall in London and enjoyed an impressive dinner at the Half-Moon Tavern in Cheapside with his fellow Masons the following day.

## Rosicrucians

It has been suggested that the esoteric Rosicrucian Order played an important part in the development of modern Masonry. The origins of the Rosicrucian movement have been debated almost as much as those of Freemasonry. Quite how the Rosicrucian movement began is something of a mystery in itself. In 1614, a Lutheran theologian named Johannes Valentin Andreae published an enigmatic pamphlet entitled *Fama Fraternitatis Rosae Crucis* or *The Fame of the Brotherhood of the Rosy Cross*. It describes how the Rosicrucian movement was founded by a German, called Christian Rosenkreuz, who was born in 1378. According to the pamphlet, Rosenkreuz had travelled to the Holy Land and come into the possession of secret occult knowledge, taught to him by a number of Eastern masters. He is then said to have founded the Rosicrucian Order in 1407 and deliberately limited its membership to eight members only. Rosenkreuz is alleged to have died in 1484 at the advanced age of 106 years old. The order was then supposed to have been kept a closely guarded secret, as its founder had wished, until it emerged on the European stage with the publication of the pamphlet. Further pamphlets followed, the *Confessio Fraternitatis* in 1615 and *The Chymical Wedding of Christian Rosen Kreuz* in 1616. Some writers and scholars have seen these documents as highly symbolic and allegorical in nature. The events they describe are not to be taken literally but need careful interpretation to reveal their true meaning.

An interesting alternative legend exists that describes the foundation of the Rosicrucian movement by a sage from the city of Alexandria called Ormus in 46 AD. This version of the origins of the movement appears to have been put forward in the eighteenth century by a Rosicrucianist-Masonic group called the Golden and Rosy Cross. The legend claims that Mark, the disciple of Jesus, converted Ormus and some of his followers to Christianity. The Rosicrucian Order, therefore, was based on a fusion of early Christian teaching and Egyptian beliefs and ideas. The story of Christian Rosenkreuz is incorporated into this series of events when he becomes the Grand Master of the existing Rosicrucian Order. It has been conjectured by some that the secret knowledge which Christian Rosenkreuz was said to have gained in the first theory of the origins of Rosicrucianism could have been absorbed into Freemasonry. Whilst travelling in the Holy Land he could have learned from the Eastern masters the stories and legends of the Temple of Solomon and, upon his return to Europe, shared that knowledge within the secret order. That knowledge could, in turn, have been transmitted to the developing Masonic orders via an initiate and become part of its rituals and iconography. Although such speculative thought has fired the interest of many, it seems that the 'emergence' of the Rosicrucian movement may, in fact, have an altogether more mundane explanation. The author of the pamphlets, Johannes Valentin Andreae, would later explain that he had intended the documents to be viewed as a kind of farce or drama designed to make an allegorical point.

As already mentioned, Andreae was a Lutheran theologian and, as a Protestant, he believed that a society freed from the restrictions and restraints of the Roman Catholic Church would be able to explore more freely such subjects as alchemy and science, thus aiding mankind in the pursuit of a new, more utopian era. However, whatever the rationale behind the pamphlets may have been, the ideas contained within them provoked much interest in seventeenth century Europe, although there is no evidence that an actual secret society existed before the publication of the papers. Freemasons certainly were interested in the ideas inherent within Rosicrucianism and, in some instances, incorporated the image of the rose and cross into their iconography. It has been suggested that there are similarities between the aims of Freemasonry and its attempts to effect a kind of spiritual, alchemical change in the world view of an individual Mason and the mystical goals of the Rosicrucian movement in developing human potential through mystical study.

In the Masonic Scottish Rite the Knight of the Rose Croix degree is the 18th degree or stage of development. In addition there exists a Masonic group called the Order of Masonic Rosicrucians that is open to Master Masons through invitation. The order focuses particularly on the Rosicrucian documents and studies them along with other mystical teachings such as the Hermetic tradition.

## Invisible College

One of the most influential groups during the renaissance period that involved active Freemasons was the so-called Invisible College. This society of scientists and philosophers was created in the seventeenth century and included amongst its members such distinguished figures as Robert Boyle, Elias Ashmole, Christopher Wren, Francis Bacon and Isaac Newton. The society offered a forum for discussion and the mutual exchange of ideas on subjects that would have included science, alchemy and assorted esoteric ideas. However, the religious and political climate of the time meant that the discussion of such issues was potentially a dangerous undertaking. Scientists such as Galileo had provoked the ire of the Roman Catholic Church by suggesting that the earth moved around the sun and those found guilty of heresy could be burned to death at the stake. In England the turmoil of the Civil War and the paranoia of Puritanism led to the appalling witch-hunts, with which that period is associated.

It was vital therefore that the exchange of such information be concealed within the framework of the Invisible College. It has been suggested that the move from operative to speculative Freemasonry may have taken place during this period because the secrecy of the operative stonemasons' guilds provided secure meeting places for such freethinkers and philosophers. By veiling their intellectual pursuits in allegory, it was possible to avoid the suspicions of the state and the Church. The Invisible College would emerge into the open when, in 1662, Charles II granted them the privilege of a royal charter. The Invisible College would form the basis for the subsequent creation of the Royal Society.

## Freemasonry after 1717

The year 1717 is a key date in the history of Freemasonry and was when the Craft became a much more publicly visible and recognised organisation. Four London lodges of Masons took the decision to form one 'Grand Lodge' that would subsequently act as the presiding head of all English Lodges. The four lodges had previously met in taverns and alehouses around the city. The Goose and Gridiron alehouse, close to St Paul's Cathedral, had been the meeting point for Lodge No.1 whilst Lodge No.2 had convened at the Crown, close to Drury Lane. The members of Lodge No.3 held their meetings at the Apple Tree Tavern in Covent Garden and Lodge No. 4 met at a tavern in Westminster called the Rummer and Grapes. The separate lodges met in the Apple Tree tavern in February 1717 where it was agreed that they would be combined to become the Grand Lodge of England or GLE. On St John the Baptist's feast day, 24 June 1717, the combined lodge met at the Goose and Gridiron and elected their first Grand Master who was called Anthony Sayer. The Grand Lodge appeared to go from strength to strength and, in 1721, altered its title to the Premier Grand Lodge of England. By that time, it could count itself the head of over 50 lodges in and around London.

They also elected the Duke of Montague as their Grand Master, which was something of a departure for a movement that had not, as a rule, previously elected individuals from the aristocracy. Dr James Anderson, a Freemason of Scottish descent, produced and had published the Constitutions of the Free-Masons in 1723. The full title of this important Masonic document is 'The Constitution, History, Laws, Charges, Orders, Regulations, and Usages, of the Right Worshipful Fraternity of Accepted Free Masons; collected from their general Records, and their faithful traditions of many Ages'. One of James Anderson's greatest innovations in his interpretation of the rules and history of Freemasonry was his shift of the religious emphasis of the Brotherhood away from a specifically Christian doctrine.

He paved the way for modern Freemasonry's more generalised concept of a universal God with the insertion of the statement that Masons should recognise 'that religion in which all men agree' and by establishing in written form the concept of a 'Great Architect of the Universe', drawing on the inherent iconography of

Freemasonry itself and the symbolism of building and design. However, Anderson's history of the order, arguing that the secrets of Freemasonry had passed from Noah and that Moses had been a Mason, has generally been accepted as imaginative invention. Anderson also concluded that Hiram Abiff had been an actual historical figure and that he had been chief architect at the building of the Temple of King Solomon exactly as Masonic lore relates.

There has been considerable speculation about the reasons for the creation of the Grand Lodge and its subsequent growth and influence and its associations with powerful and aristocratic members of society. In their book *The Temple and the Lodge*, authors Michael Baigent and Richard Leigh argue that it was a consequence of the Jacobite revolution of 1715 that ended in failure and the retaining of power in England by the House of Hanover. Because Freemasonry had strong links with Scotland and, in the authors' opinion, was inseparable from the Stuart cause, there was fear that it could be seen as a threat to the English monarchy. In France, where many Jacobites had sought shelter in previous years, evidence suggests that Freemasonry was in favour of the restoration of the Stuarts in England. By forming the Grand Lodge, English Masons were attempting to take an impartial stance. They were stressing that they were neither politically nor religiously partisan and aligning themselves with the establishment of the day. By placing high-ranking members of the aristocracy in its most senior positions, Freemasonry was effectively declaring that it posed no disruptive threat to society. In the next few decades Ireland and Scotland followed suit, forming their own Grand Lodges.

During this period, Freemasonry continued to develop into the form in which it is recognised today. A notable example of this development is the introduction of the Third Degree of Master Mason in around 1725. The ritual of the Third Degree is thought by some to have been instigated by a former Grand Master named John Theophilus Desaguliers. The Third Degree of the Master Mason was officially accepted by the Grand Lodge in 1738 when Anderson's revised Constitutions were accepted. Although the Grand Lodge of England had grown in status, there remained large groups of Masons that operated outside the influence of the newly created body. These 'Old Masons' tended to be from working class backgrounds and felt a sense of separation from the increasingly aristocratic nature of the Grand Lodge of England. Many Irish and Scottish Masons felt that they had little in common with the reconstituted GLE which had, they believed, moved away from what they considered to be an 'ancient' and more authentic form of Freemasonry.

The working class Masons of London forged greater links with Scottish and Irish Masons in London until, on 17 July 1751, a rival Grand Lodge was constituted. Members of five different lodges assembled in the Turk's

Head Tavern, at that time located on Greek Street in Soho, and took the step of forming an alternative body to the GLE which they called 'The Most Ancient and Honourable Society of Free and Accepted Masons'. Because of their belief that they represented an older, more undiluted form of Freemasonry they referred to themselves as 'the Ancients' and dubbed the Grand Lodge of England 'the Moderns'.

The formation of the rival Grand Lodge appeared to create a schism within English Masonry for over half a century, although later Masonic historians were quick to point out that the majority of those belonging to the Ancients were, in fact, Irish rather than English. However, in 1813, the two factions were finally reconciled and the two groups were merged together to create the United Grand Lodge of England. The new body thus formed from the rival groups tended to favour the Ancients' approach to Masonic ceremonies and rituals.

## The French Revolution

Authors Michael Baigent and Richard Leigh have suggested that Freemasonry first arrived in France between 1688 and 1691 with what remained of the Jacobite army of James II. However, the first reliable and unequivocal documentation for the founding of a French Masonic lodge dates from 1725. It is known that, in 1728, a number of French lodges formed the English

Grand Lodge of France. The first Grand Master of the newly created body was the Duke of Wharton who had previously served as the Grand Master of the Grand Lodge of England. In 1737, as we have already seen in Chapter 5, Andrew Michael Ramsay delivered the famous 'Ramsay Oration' in Paris. His argument that Freemasonry had its origins in the Holy Land at the time of the crusades and that it had survived in Scotland right through to the eighteenth century proved to be very popular and influential in France.

However, in 1737, King Louis XV of France banned Freemasonry amidst paranoid anxiety that it might serve as a source of secret plotting amongst the aristocracy against him. The Catholic Church was also, and remains today, strongly opposed to Freemasonry and, whilst it flourished in Protestant England, it was attacked by the Vatican. The first Papal condemnation of Freemasonry was issued on 28 April 1738 by Pope Clement XII. In his papal bull Clement stated that:

Now it has come to Our ears, and common gossip has made clear, that certain Societies, Companies, Assemblies, Meetings, Congregations or Conventicles called in the popular tongue Liberi Muratori or Francs Massons or by other names according to the various languages, are spreading far and wide and daily growing in strength: and men of any Religion or sect, satisfied with the appearance of natural probity, are joined together, according to the laws and the statutes laid down for them, by a strict and unbreakable bond which obligates them, both by an oath upon the Holy Bible and by a host of grievous punishments, to an inviolable silence about all that they do in secret together. But it is in the nature of the crime to betray itself and show itself by its attendant clamour. Thus these aforesaid Societies or Conventicles have caused in the minds of the faithful the greatest suspicion, and all prudent and upright men have passed the same judgement on them as being depraved and perverted.

Despite the ban of 1737, and the fact that Pope Clement XII also condemned Freemasonry and threatened excommunication to any who joined it in his papal bull of 1738, the Craft continued to thrive and grow in France. Many Masonic lodges in France followed the Ancient Scottish Rite that Ramsay popularised. In 1756, French Masonry was divided when the English Grand Lodge of France declared itself to be completely independent and renamed itself as the Grand Lodge of France. Just as the formation of the United Grand Lodge of England had led to a schism within English Masonry, so the decision to reorganise the structure of French Masonry led to a split between 'ancients' and 'moderns'. The Grand Lodge of France renamed itself as the Grand Orient of France in 1772 and also altered its statutes, a move that led to further dissent within French Freemasonry. Perhaps predictably, some Masons refused to acknowledge these changes and continued under the original name and with the original statutes.

However, events were to take a more dramatic turn with the death of King Louis XV in 1774 and the ascension to the French throne of his grandson Louis XVI. His reign was marked by a series of financial disasters and excess which provided his own circle with wealth whilst the people of France experienced poverty and deprivation. Events would lead Louis XVI to hold a meeting of the Estates-General in 1788 that consisted of individuals from the Church, or First Estate, the aristocracy, the Second Estate, and the middle classes, the Third Estate. The Third Estate refused to accept the influence of the other two groups and assumed the leadership of France.

The French Revolution is often seen as beginning with the storming of the Bastille, which took place on 14 July 1789 when it was believed that Louis XVI intended to dissolve the assembly and challenge the power of the Third Estate. Many within the assembly were, in fact, Freemasons. Louis was later tried for conspiring with Austrian forces and sentenced to death. It has been estimated that as many as 320 of the total of 1,336 members of the assembly were Freemasons. In the wake of the Revolution, many claimed that Freemasonry had been responsible for the turmoil and violence that had rocked French society.

However, Freemasonry had actually declined in popularity during the French Revolution and, in many cases, lodges were suspended. Many of those involved in the initial move to revolution were Freemasons and, as noted in Chapter One, they took their famous proclamation of 'Liberty, Equality, Fraternity' from basic

Masonic principles. In many ways it is ironic that Freemasonry became associated with revolutionary activities in France (and in North America and, later, Central and South America) because, according to Masonic teaching, one of the key duties of a Mason is to maintain law and order and to keep political opinions to themselves. The earliest Masonic charges or rules declare Masons must not plot or otherwise conspire against the King or government. This principle is clearly stated in the revised constitutions of Dr Anderson used by the Grand Lodge of England. The rift that had occurred in French Freemasonry, creating the divergent groups of Ancient and Moderns, was finally ended in 1799. They became reconciled through an Act of Union and the Grand Lodge of France became part of the Grand Orient of France.

Perhaps surprisingly, Freemasonry in France was to thrive and grow during the reign of the Emperor Napoleon Bonaparte. Initially, he regarded Freemasonry as a form of secret society and therefore a potential threat to his power, and he feared that it might shelter and nurture insurrectionary elements. He issued a decree, stating that official permission must be granted for any assembly of over 20 people and had investigations carried out into whether Freemasonry posed a threat to his rule. When his agents reported that Masons were not harbouring any political plans against him, his suspicions were allayed and the Craft was allowed to flourish. Interestingly, Napoleon's first wife, Josephine, was closely involved in a Masonic-style group. She was the Grand Mistress of the Saint Caroline Lodge of Adoption.

During the late 1870s a major split occurred between French and English Freemasons on religious grounds. Whilst Freemasons are drawn from a variety of religious backgrounds, it is traditionally, and according to Dr Anderson's constitutions, a prerequisite that they express a belief in God and that a Mason will 'never be a stupid atheist'. The Grand Orient of France took what was perceived in England as the dramatic step of admitting atheists and agnostics into its ranks. The ritual of entry into the Brotherhood was adapted by the Grand Orient of France and the Masonic phrase that refers to God as the Supreme Being or the Great Architect was removed. The Grand Orient of France also caused consternation amongst Freemasons in other countries when it declared that it would involve itself more directly in politics. But protests from abroad failed to move the governing body of French Masonry and the Grand Orient of France was declared to be irregular by other Grand Lodges. The situation was only rectified in 1913 with the formation of the National Grand Lodge of France.

## The Bavarian Illuminati

Freemasonry was linked to other revolutionary causes in Europe during the eighteenth century. On 1 May 1776, a lay professor called Adam Weishaupt founded a movement which referred to itself as the 'Perfectibilists' but its members became better known as the Illuminati or the 'Illuminated ones'. Originally the order consisted of only five members but it reached a peak of 2,500 members during its existence. It was based in Ingolstadt in Upper Bavaria. The alleged aim of the order was dramatic: to effect revolution by bringing to an end existing world governments and replacing them with a new order based on freedom and tolerance. It drew many of its members from Freemasonry but was not officially sanctioned by the brotherhood.

It had a Masonic-style structure, being organised into three primary groups that developed in seniority of position. The first stage within the Illuminati was known as Novice, the second as Minerval whilst the third was designated as the Minerval Illumine, or Master. Although its internal structure held obvious parallels with Freemasonry, a major distinction between the two movements was that membership of the Illuminati did not require any belief in a God or Supreme Being. A consequence of this disparity between the two groups was that many atheists were drawn to the Order. The Order became effectively illegal when the Bavarian government, led by Karl Theodor, moved to ban any form of secret society in 1785. The ban applied to both Freemasons and the Illuminati. The adherents of the Illuminati viewed themselves as enlightened freethinkers and included artists, politicians and writers as well as many members from aristocratic backgrounds.

# Freemasonry in America

The new world of America was to prove an extremely fertile ground in which Freemasonry could take root. It has been argued that many in the old world of Europe saw in the apparently unspoiled nature of the newly discovered continent an opportunity to establish ideal utopian societies free from the mistakes of the past. As we have seen, Rosicrucianism and its attendant beliefs in perfecting the human soul and working towards an idealised new age of human affairs exerted a powerful influence on the development of Freemasonry. In this sense America, unfettered by the restraints of the Roman Catholic Church, presented enormous scope for the spread and influence of Freemasonic societies. Information on the early growth of Freemasonry in America is sketchy but the movement of people and ideas from Europe clearly meant that it would be inevitable that, at some point, the Craft would be carried there.

The first known Freemason to settle in America, one whose membership of the Brotherhood is verifiable by contemporary written records, was a man called John

Skene. He is thought to have been born around 1649 and his parents Alexander Skene and Lilias Gillespie lived in the English town of Newtyle. Skene is recorded as being a Mason within a lodge in Aberdeen in 1670. In 1682, he emigrated to America where he settled his family on a plantation in New Jersey. Skene appears to have achieved success in his newly adopted country and rose to the rank of deputy colonial governor for West Jersey. However, lack of surviving evidence makes it seem unlikely (although not impossible) that Skene created or participated in any Freemasonic activity in America. The first recorded settler born in America who became a Freemason was Andrew Belcher. In 1704, he was inducted into a lodge whilst in England. In 1733 the first American lodge to receive an official warrant from the Grand Lodge of England was St John's Lodge of Boston. Masonic lodges were also in evidence in America within military lodges of the British Army that conducted their ceremonies and meetings in the field.

Benjamin Franklin played a major role in the promotion of Freemasonry in America through his work in newspapers such as the Pennsylvania Gazette. Franklin became a Mason in 1732 and became junior warden of the Pennsylvania Grand Lodge in the same year. It has been argued that the lodge system in America provided a forum for the discussion of views at this time and also served to a great extent as a unifying factor for the colonies. Franklin became an outspoken defender of American rights against the controls of the British government and he would, of course, play a major role in the foundation of the emerging nation.

## Boston Tea Party

The Boston Tea Party is today remembered as one of the most important events leading to the American Revolution and the achievement of independence from British rule. American Freemasons were directly involved in this symbolic act of defiance. A small party of men, who had concealed their identities by dressing as Mohawk Indians, stole aboard a British ship on 16 December 1773. The merchant ship named the Dartmouth was the property of the British East India Company. Once on board the men proceeded to throw its load of 32 chests of tea into Boston's harbour. The value of the tea was estimated at 10,000 pounds. The purpose of this seemingly bizarre act of sabotage was to protest against taxation on tea and, more generally, against British taxation without democratic representation. It is claimed that the raid was formulated in the 'Long Room' of Freemasons' Hall, an establishment that had previously been a tavern called the Green Dragon. The group who carried out the raid were known as the 'Sons of Liberty' but Freemasons were amongst their number. Twelve members of St Andrew's Lodge, Boston, participated in the Tea Party. It is worthy of note that a further twelve later became Freemasons following this act of subversion.

## The American Revolution

George Washington led the largely untrained colonial army against the British forces. Washington was born in Virginia in 1732 and had been made a Freemason in 1753 when he was initiated into the Fredericksburg lodge. In 1788, he became the charter master of a lodge in Alexandria. However, although Washington, like many of the generals of the colonial army, was a Mason, it appears that he was not particularly closely involved in lodge activities. Whilst Washington led the conflict, Franklin travelled to France to seek aid. In 1777, he was initiated into the Lodge des Neuf Souers or the Lodge of the Nine Sisters in Paris. The following year he helped initiate Voltaire into the lodge. The friendship between the two men helped sway the sympathy of the French people towards the American cause.

As has already been noted, there were Freemasons on both sides at the time of the American Revolution. An interesting and unusual example of a Native American Indian becoming a Freemason is the Mohawk war leader Joseph Brant, known as Thayendanegea in his own language. Brant visited Britain in 1775 in order to represent the Mohawk people, who were fighting on the side of the British, and to ensure that the British Crown and its officials would make good their promises of protection when the conflict ceased. During the 1770s, Brant had risen to the rank of captain in the British army. Upon his visit to England he was inducted into a Masonic lodge and mixed with a number of notable figures from English society such as James Boswell and Hugh Percy, 2nd Duke of Northumberland. Today, the Masonic apron that the lodge gave to him is held at Barton lodge in Hamilton, Ontario. Upon his return to America he was involved in fighting with the rebels and the British later handed the Mohawks prisoners for torture. It is reported that when a number of prisoners made Masonic signs he had them freed.

## American Declaration of Independence

When the Declaration of Independence was published by Congress in 1776, 15 of the 56 signers were Freemasons or likely to have been members. It has been argued that the ideals and values of Freemasonry also exerted a powerful influence over the formulation of the American Constitution. The constitution was confirmed on 13 September 1788. It is known that 28 of the 40 signers of this document were either definitely Masons or likely to have been members of the Brotherhood. George Washington and Benjamin Franklin were known to be Masons, as were John Blair, John Dickinson, Rufus King, Gunning Bedford Junior, David Brearly, Daniel Carrol and Jacob Broom. Interestingly, a further number of the signers of the constitution became Freemasons at a later date.

George Washington was elected as the first president of the United States of America on 4 February 1789.

When Washington took the presidential oath of office on 30 April 1789, the ceremony was administered by Robert Livingstone, the Grand Master of New York's Grand Lodge. (Benjamin Franklin died on 17 April 1789 and therefore did not live to see the inauguration of George Washington.) Freemasons also played a major role when Washington laid the cornerstone of the Capitol on 18 September 1793. A great procession was held and included the Grand Lodge of Maryland, with Washington acting as its master, together with members of his own lodge from Alexandria, Virginia. The Grand Lodge of Maryland was accompanied by other lodges that were affiliated to it.

A silver plate had been specially made for the occasion that carried the designations of the lodges present. After a group of artillery had fired a ceremonial volley into the air Washington stepped down into a trench in which the south-east cornerstone was set. He put the commemorative silver plate on top of the stone. Washington also set offerings of corn, oil and wine in jars in the trench and, as we have seen, all these are important symbols within Masonic rituals. The assembled gathering of Freemasons offered prayers that were followed by a second volley of shots into the air.

After he had laid the offerings in the trench, Washington ascended a small rostrum with three steps common to Masonic ritual and addressed the assembly. The authors Michael Baigent and Richard Leigh, in their book *The Temple and the Lodge*, contend that the White

House and the Capitol formed the basis of a geometrical design for the city of Washington that has Masonic significance. They argue that George Washington and Thomas Jefferson planned them as the focal centres of octagonal patterns whose shape incorporates the specific cross that Masonic Templars use in their symbolism.

## Washington National Memorial

An important Masonic landmark within the capital city of Washington is the House of the Temple. This temple serves as the headquarters of the Supreme Council, 33 degrees, Ancient and Accepted Scottish Rite of Freemasonry, Southern Jurisdiction of America. The cornerstone of the building was put in place on 18 October 1911 and the ceremony of dedication marking its completion occurred on 18 October 1915. The temple is also the final resting place of the Civil War general Albert Pike who was hugely influential in popularising the Scottish Rite within the Southern Jurisdiction of American Freemasonry. The architecture of the House of the Temple was based on the Mausoleum of Mausolos, one of the Seven Wonders of the Ancient World.

## Prince Hall Freemasonry

The first African American to become a Freemason was a man called Prince Hall who was initiated into the Irish

Constitution Military Lodge in Boston Massachusetts in 1775. Prince Hall became a Freemason with 14 other 'free born' African-Americans. Although few details have survived about the life of Prince Hall, some claim that he was born on 12 September 1748 in Barbados. He may have been a slave in Boston and been freed in 1770. He is believed to have fought in the Revolutionary War. After being initiated as Freemasons, Prince Hall and 14 other African American men applied for a Lodge Warrant from the Premier Grand Lodge of England. Their application was successful and they went on to form African Lodge, Number 459 (Premier Grand Lodge of England) in 1787.

Under the conditions of the Premier Grand Lodge of England, the newly established African Lodge was able to give permission for the foundation of other lodges with itself as the head lodge. Subsequently, further African Lodges came into being in other American cities such as New York. In 1791, Prince Hall became the Grand Master of the African Grand Lodge of North America and, following his death in 1807, the name of the lodge was changed to the Prince Hall Grand Lodge of Massachusetts in 1808 as a tribute to him. During his life Hall was active in promoting the foundation of schools for black children from Boston. The African Lodge of Boston became independent from the Grand Lodge of England in 1827. It is recognised that the African American Prince Hall Freemasons contributed greatly to the education of black men and women both within their lodges and also by providing funds for college scholarships. Today, Prince Hall lodges like most Masonic lodges are open to a multi-ethnic background.

## The Scottish Rite

As we have seen, Freemasonry was to flourish in America and two further systems of Masonic degrees have been adopted to allow Master Masons to learn more about the Craft. For those who have achieved the first three stages of blue lodge Masonic development, that is Entered Apprentice, Fellowcraft and Master Mason, the Scottish Rite offers an opportunity for candidates to progress within a framework of a further 30 degrees. However, the final degree, the 33rd degree, cannot be applied for by individuals but is bestowed on Masons who are thought to have made a particularly significant contribution to the world of Freemasonry or the Scottish Rite in particular or who are deemed to have performed some exceptional service to humanity. The Scottish Rite is recognised by American Grand Lodges as an extension of the traditional three degrees. In England it is not officially recognised by the Grand Lodge but Freemasons are not prevented from undertaking it.

There has been considerable speculation about the development of the Scottish Rite. It has been suggested by authors Michael Baigent and Richard Leigh and by other commentators that this particular branch of Freemasonry was influenced by and inseparably linked to the Jacobite cause of the seventeenth and eighteenth centuries. In America the Scottish Rite proved to be an outstanding success and, in South Carolina, the Supreme Council of the Ancient and Accepted Scottish Rite was established in 1801, the first such council of the Scottish Rite to be founded. The popularity and success of the Scottish Rite within the history of the Southern Jurisdiction of American Freemasonry is very often attributed to the Civil War general and Freemason Albert Pike. Pike was born in Boston, Massachusetts on 29 December 1809. He received the fourth to thirty-second degrees in Charleston in 1853 and the thirty-third in 1857 in New Orleans.

Today the Scottish Rite within America is governed by two Supreme Councils. The Supreme Council of the Southern Jurisdiction is based in Washington, DC, whilst the Supreme Council of the Northern Masonic Jurisdiction is located in Lexington, Massachusetts. Masons working through the different degrees of the Scottish Rite meet in groups known as 'Valleys' over which the Supreme Council has particular authority.

The first ten degrees within the Scottish Rite are known as the Ineffable Degrees and are:

4th degree    Secret Master
In this degree the candidate learns that in order to fulfil his duties it is at times necessary to be able to keep

secrets and remain trustworthy. The imagery and allegorical content of this degree derives from a story
concerning the Temple of Solomon and seven Masons
appointed to protect the holy of holies.

### 5th degree    Perfect Master

This degree addresses the transience of human life but
teaches the importance of revering and respecting our
forbears and stresses the need to behave honourably. The
murder of Hiram Abiff is an important part of the
symbolism in the degree of Perfect Master.

### 6th degree    Intimate Secretary

Masons are instructed that they should not involve
themselves unduly in the affairs of their fellow Masons
and the degree is based on a story about King Solomon
intervening to protect a Mason accused of spying.

### 7th degree    Provost and Judge

This degree teaches the importance of fairness and
equality within any system of justice and that Masons
should behave honourably and mercifully. Its symbolic
context is the trial of the murderers of Hiram Abiff.

### 8th degree    Intendant of the Building

The theme of the Intendant of the Building is charity and
helping the less fortunate in society and its allegorical
backdrop is the resumption of the construction of the
Temple of Solomon after the murder of Hiram Abiff.

9th degree    Elect of the Nine
The title of the degree refers to King Solomon choosing nine Masons to find the murderers of Hiram Abiff. It teaches the importance of serving others within society.

10th degree    Elect of the Fifteen
The 10th degree of the Scottish Rite instructs candidates that justice will triumph in the end over unfair and unrighteous actions. Its symbolic context is the trial of the murderers of Hiram Abiff.

11th degree    Elect of the Twelve
The 11th degree is intended to show Masons that those who show honesty and fairness and behave with honour will reap the rewards of their actions just as unbecoming or corrupt actions will result in punishment through fair and impartial justice.

12th degree    Grand Master Architect
The degree of Grand Master Architect uses the allegorical symbolism of the education of the builders of the Temple of King Solomon to instruct Masons in their role within the world and to respect the work of the Great Architect.

13th degree    Royal Arch of Solomon
This degree concerns the difficulties and hardships that may face a Mason in striving for perfection. It teaches that the achievement of high goals is through persistent

and, at times, difficult struggle and labour.

14th degree    Grand Elect Perfect and Sublime
It is believed that a Mason, once he has reached this stage within the Scottish Rite, has been fully prepared to construct his own metaphorical lodge of perfection. In this degree the candidate discovers that a hidden chamber under the Temple of Solomon was built to house a precious artefact referred to as the pillar of beauty.

The next sequence of degrees is called the Chapter of Rose Croix. The symbolic context in which moral lessons are taught to Masons is the captivity of the Jews in Babylon and their eventual release and return to Jerusalem:

15th degree    Knight of the East or Sword
Candidates learn that it is essential to retain their integrity and beliefs and not to be dissuaded from them.

16th degree    Prince of Jerusalem
When the Jews returned to Jerusalem they undertook the building of the Second Temple and faced hardship, often having to fight for their freedom. Masons learn that they must meet their responsibilities even in the face of hardship and danger.

17th degree    Knight of the East and West
This degree acknowledges the lesson that the lasting

Temple to the Great Architect lies not in the material world but within the spiritual world.

18th degree    Knight Rose Croix
The ultimate degree of the Chapter of Rose Croix instructs Masons to build a temple to God within themselves and concerns the Rosicrucian themes of transforming society through the transformation of our own souls.

The next stage within the Scottish Rite is referred to as the Council of Kadosh and runs from the 19th to the 30th:

19th degree    Grand Pontiff
The theme of the degree of Grand Pontiff is that the Mason should look beyond individual creeds and religions and that those who believe in a divine power and the immortality of the soul are as one.

20th degree    Master ad Vitam
Master ad Vitam deals with the problems and requirements of leadership. It stresses the importance of individuals working together to improve society.

21st degree    Patriarch Noachite
This degree emphasises that Masons must not abuse their position within Freemasonry and must behave honourably and within the law. It also teaches respect for justice correctly and fairly administered.

22nd degree    Prince of Libanus

The 22nd degree takes its title from an ancient name for the country of Lebanon. In the story of the building of the Temple of Solomon cedar wood used in its construction came from Lebanon. The degree teaches the value and the honour inherent in hard work through the allegorical framework of cutting wood.

23rd degree    Chief of the Tabernacle

The Mason is reminded to strive always to give aid to their fellows and to perform good works in recognition of the Great Architect.

24th degree    Prince of the Tabernacle

The degree of Prince of the Tabernacle is aimed to illustrate how peoples around the world, apparently from differing cultures, actually have much in common. Through the study of symbolism Masons must learn to recognise these universal concerns and promote co-operation and mutual aid and respect.

25th degree    Knight of the Brazen Serpent

This degree recognises that all people must suffer hardships but that good will triumph over evil.

26th degree    Prince of Mercy

The subject of this degree is showing mercy and understanding to others even if they have offended or wronged us. Justice and any accompanying punishment should be administered with this in mind.

27th degree    Commander of the Temple
The 27th degree is based on what is known of the
crusading order known as the Teutonic Knights of the
House of St Mary of Jerusalem. The Order performed
the dual function of providing medical assistance and
serving as warriors.

28th degree    Knight of the Sun
The degree of the Knight of the Sun is strongly influ-
enced by the Kabbalah and the concept of the Tree of
Life.

29th degree    Knight of St Andrew
The Mason is shown the importance of treating the ideas
and beliefs of others with respect and the degree
encourages a spirit of tolerance within humanity.

30th degree    Knight Kadosh
The Knight Kadosh is the final degree in the Council of
Kadosh and teaches that the difficulties that we face
improve us as people and that Masons must strive to
protect the metaphorical internal temple within themselves that they have built through their Masonic
training.

31st degree    Inspector Inquisitor Commander
The subject of this degree is justice and the recognition

that all people must judge their own weaknesses and failings before judging others. Once again fair and appropriate justice must be accompanied with compassion and understanding.

32nd degree    Sublime Prince of the Royal Secret
The 32nd degree examines the difference in human nature between our physical selves and our spiritual beings. It teaches that the spiritual can overcome selfishness and self-interest through struggle and that Masons may have to make great sacrifices to help others.

33rd degree    Knight Commander of the Court of Honour
As noted earlier in this chapter, the 33rd degree is an honorary degree and can only be given by fellow Masons, usually for an outstanding achievement or contribution.

## The York Rite

The York Rite also offers an opportunity for Master Masons to progress further within the world of Freemasonry beyond the standard three degrees of Blue Lodge Masonry. The York Rite is found mainly as a single system in America and there are differences within the different Orders that teach it. Within the York Rite a Master Mason is firstly eligible to join the order known as Royal Arch Masonry, also referred to as the Chapter, indicating a group of Royal Arch Masons. The second body within the York Rite is the Council of Royal and Select Masters, often referred to as Cryptic Masonry. It derives this secondary term of identification because some form of underground chamber or crypt-like room forms a part of the developing degrees that it encompasses. The third and final body within the York Rite is that of Knights Templar.

Within Royal Arch Masonry candidates may undertake the Mark Master Mason degree. It takes its name and symbolism from the practice of medieval Masons carving individual symbols upon the structures and stonework for which they were responsible in order that they might be recognised by other Masons. The next degree within Royal Arch Masonry is that of Virtual Past Master. This is followed by the degree of Most Excellent Master and is unique within Freemasonry in that its imagery is of the completion of King Solomon's Temple. The final degree in the sequence is that of the Royal Arch Mason and this is very often termed the 'most beautiful', sublime or elegant degree within Freemasonry. Those who reach this elevated Masonic degree are eligible, but not obliged, to undertake the degrees of Cryptic Masonry. The degrees within the Cryptic Rite are that of Royal Master, Select Master and Super Excellent Master.

The last part of the York Rite, known as the Commandery of Knights Templar, is unusual in Masonic groups in that its membership does require a specific religious belief system. Whilst Freemasonry in general is open to individuals with a belief in a supreme being, the degree of Knights Templar is only open to Master Masons whose religion is Christianity.

## William Morgan

Freemasonry had grown exponentially in America but it was dealt a major blow in 1826 with the mysterious case of the disappearance of a man called William Morgan. He was from Culpepper County in Virginia and had travelled to Canada to find work, eventually taking up residence in the town of Batavia in New York State. Records show that Morgan was awarded the Royal Arch degree in the Western Star Chapter No. 33 of Le Roy on 31 May 1825. Sources differ as to how he became involved in Freemasonry and some within the brotherhood allege deception and dishonesty. Morgan was then amongst a group of Freemasons from Batavia who sought permission to establish a Royal Arch chapter. Although they were successful in their aim, Morgan himself was later rejected by his fellow Masons. This rejection led him to attack the order by claiming that he had written a book that would expose important Masonic secrets to the general public. He also claimed that he had signed a contract for the publication of this book, exposing the inner workings of Freemasonry, that would involve a payment to him of a colossal for the time figure of 500,000 dollars.

The publishers of the book were said to include a man

called David C Miller who, like Morgan, was a disgruntled Freemason and two others. Morgan was reportedly extremely vocal about the book and caused considerable consternation within the Brotherhood. Events took a sinister turn when he was arrested in September 1826 for a dubious and unlikely minor offence; he was alleged to have stolen a shirt and tie. Although the charge came to nothing he was actually jailed for having failed to pay an outstanding debt of a few dollars. Morgan was to spend only a single day imprisoned as a mysterious and still unknown benefactor settled the amount he owed. However, as soon as he was released, it was reported that a small group of men forced him to accompany them away from the jail in a coach. The men apparently took him to a disused fort where they detained him.

The news of the apparent abduction of William Morgan led to feverish speculation that he had been taken by Freemasons who had killed him to prevent their secrets being revealed. When a body was discovered on the banks of the river Niagara it was at first thought that it must be that of the kidnapped Morgan. The corpse was initially identified by Morgan's own wife because it was wearing Morgan's clothes. On closer inspection the identification was questioned because marks and scars on the body did not match those known to be on William Morgan's. After three separate inquests, it was established that the body actually belonged to a Canadian man called Timothy Munro who was identified by his wife, Sara.

The mystery of the fate of William Morgan had mean-while remained unresolved. Seven men, all known to be Masons, were subsequently arrested for the kidnapping of Morgan but charges of murder were never made because of the absence of an identifiable body. The fate of the abducted man has never been conclusively proved but, at the time, the news of his apparent abduction by a band of Freemasons trying to prevent the secret work-ings of their order being made public, sent shockwaves of fear across America. Suddenly Freemasons were regarded as a sinister and evil force at work within American society. In the immediate aftermath of the kidnapping anti-Masonic feelings ran high. The Church condemned Masons, individuals were forced out of their jobs for being Masons, newspapers such as the Anti-Masonic Review were founded and there was a signifi-cant decrease in the number of Masonic candidates and Lodges across America.

# Freemasonry in the Modern Era

Whilst a diverse and famous range of individuals including such figures as Winston Churchill, Oscar Wilde and John Wayne have been Freemasons, its public image in the modern era has very often been a negative one. Conspiracy theories implicating Masonry in plans for world domination have abounded and Freemasons have very often found themselves at the receiving end of bigotry and intolerance.

## Leo Taxil

The reputation of Freemasonry was dealt a serious blow in the late nineteenth century by the so-called exposés of one Gabriel Jogand-Poges writing under the pseudonym of Leo Taxil. Born in 1854 in the French city of Marseilles, Jogand-Poges became a journalist and, after moving to Paris, produced a newspaper that focussed largely on scandal and intrigue. He also wrote a number of contentious books with a similar slant and content and titles like *The Secret Lovers of Pope Pius IX*. He became a Freemason in 1881 but was eventually rejected by the brotherhood. Subsequently Jogand-Poges adopted Catholicism and, perhaps inspired by the Catholic hatred of Freemasonry, wrote a number of books exposing the secrets of Masonry. Entitled *The Secret Revelations of French Masonry*, the books portrayed Freemasons as satanic devil worshippers who engaged in the most appalling and debased behaviour during their rituals.

The books of Leo Taxil were to prove an incredible popular success throughout Europe. His works on Freemasonry were also particularly anti-Semitic in their content and his vivid descriptions of Masonic secret ceremonies were fantastical and demonic. Taxil insisted that the punishment for Masons who betrayed the secrets of the Brotherhood was, potentially, death and that all Masons, as part of their oath or charge of allegiance, must be ready to commit murder. Whilst many within Freemasonry objected publicly to his distortion of the image of the Brotherhood, he was, perhaps not surprisingly, supported in his attack on the Craft by the Catholic Church. The pope of the day, Leo XIII, went so far as to award Leo Taxil the special honour of the Order of the Holy Sepulchre as a reward for his attacks on Freemasonry.

## Women in Freemasonry

Although Freemasonry has traditionally been dominated by men there are Masonic bodies that are open to women. An interesting example of a woman being admitted to a Masonic lodge at a time when Masonry was essentially a male-only affair is the case of Elizabeth St Leger. It is said that, in 1713, Elizabeth had witnessed a lodge meeting in session at the house of her father who was first Viscount Doneraile in the Irish County of Cork. Although it might seem unusual for a lodge meeting to have taken place in her father's house it was apparently normal at that time and the lodge in question had a warrant from the Grand Lodge of Ireland. It is said that she took a brick from an internal wall and was able to see into the room where the lodge was meeting. Her presence was detected and it was decided that the best course of action was to make her a Mason. She was active within Masonry during her life and was apparently treated as an equal within the fraternity. Upon her death, she is said to have received full Masonic honours at her funeral.

However, the admittance of women into Freemasonry did not begin widely until 1882 in France when Maria Deraismes became a Mason, joining the Loge Libre Penseurs, or 'Freethinkers Lodge'. This lodge was under the jurisdiction of the Grand Independent Symbolic Lodge and had broken away from the Supreme Council of France. When the Grand Lodge discovered this, they suspended Les Libres Penseurs. However, in 1892, Maria Deraismes was approached by a member of the Supreme Council called Dr Georges Martin who suggested that they found a lodge that would be open to both men and women. They established a lodge called Le Droit

Humain, or 'the Human Duty' and initiated 16 women into its ranks together with male Masons. Over the course of the next few years its popularity grew and, in 1907, the Order extended the three degrees that it had offered to include the 33 degrees of the Ancient and Accepted Scottish Rite.

In Britain, the concept of mixed Masonry was, arguably, most successfully established by Annie Besant of the Theosophical Society. Members of the Theosophical Society were also drawn to the idea of what was initially known as 'Joint Freemasonry' and later 'Universal Co-Freemasonry'. Le Droit Humain and the Order of International Co-Masonry are still in existence today. However, the United Grand Lodge of England, whilst recognising and acknowledging orders of mixed Masonry, does not allow women to become members of its particular Masonic order.

In the United States of America, the Order of the Eastern Star was formed in 1850 and its members were (and are) drawn mainly from Masons and the female relatives of Master Masons. The Order of the Eastern Star was founded by Dr Robert Morris who was himself a Former Past Grand Master of Kentucky. Initially, Dr Morris had planned to develop a form of Women's Freemasonry but the idea proved so unpopular amongst Male Masons that the compromise position of mixed Masonry was adopted. The headquarters of the Order is in Washington, DC, and housed in the Eastern Star Temple. In order to be eligible for membership a woman must currently be over the age of 18 and be the wife, daughter, widow, sister, half-sister, mother, step-mother, grand-daughter, niece or grandmother of a Master Mason.

An interesting variation on Freemasonry is the Order of Weavers, a women's group that has Masonic links but, instead of basing its moral and philosophical lessons and rituals on symbols drawn from Stonemasonry, makes use of ideas and images from the practice of weaving.

## The Golden Dawn

Freemasonry, along with Rosicrucian thought and the influence of the Theosophical Society, was to play an important role in the emergence of the magical order known as the Golden Dawn. Founded in 1887, the order was secretive in nature and consisted of both male and female members. The order began with three founding members, William Wynn Westcott, Samuel Liddell MacGregor and Dr William Robert Woodman. All three were Freemasons and were also linked to the Masonic-style group Societas Rosicruciana in Anglia, or the SRIA. As is the case with Freemasonry, the Golden Dawn was organised around a system of degrees of ascending initiation. Within the order of the Golden Dawn there were 14 different degrees. The order was strongly influenced by Hermetic thought and its members were instructed in such subjects as alchemy and the Kabbalistic tradition.

The members of the Golden Dawn believed that they constituted an elite and developed an elaborate system of personal development, reflected in the fact that their training featured so many degrees of initiation. Whilst Freemasonry was a movement that was well known within its respective societies (or, some might argue, at least maintained a public image that was widely recognised within those societies), knowledge of the existence of the order of the Golden Dawn was limited. Its most famous members included Aleister Crowley, WB Yeats and Dion Fortune.

## The Holocaust

It has been estimated that as many as 80,000 to 200,000 Freemasons were killed by the Nazi regime during the Second World War. In his autobiography *Mein Kampf* Hitler declared that Freemasonry had 'succumbed' to the Jews. He argued further that Freemasonry represented an 'excellent instrument' for the Jews to manipulate and shape society. For Hitler the 'general pacifist paralysis of the national instinct of self-preservation' of Germany following the First World War was directly attributable to Freemasonry.

It is also a little known fact that the famous American industrialist, Henry Ford, best known for the production of automobiles, was strongly anti-Semitic and also viewed the Freemasons as being part of a Jewish conspiracy to control the United States of America. Ford gave his own personal stamp of approval to a 1922 edition of an anti-Semitic piece of propaganda called *The Protocols of the Elders of Zion* by writing an introduction to it. He also aired his prejudices in the *Dearborn Independent*, his own weekly journal. He used it as a platform to publish a long series of splenetic, paranoid outbursts against Jewish people and their influence in America. Whilst the titles of Ford's diatribes, ranging from 'Jewish Gamblers Corrupt American Baseball' to 'Jewish Jazz Becomes our National Music', may have seemed almost comically hysterical, their content was unrelentingly sinister and filled with hate.

Such was the scale of the obsessive outpourings from his journal on the subject that he finally had the articles compiled into book form with the repugnant title of *The International Jew: The World's Foremost Problem*. The book became a bestseller both in America and abroad. It comes as little surprise to discover that it was greeted with great personal enthusiasm by Adolf Hitler himself. Such was Hitler's regard for Henry Ford that he is said to have kept a picture of him in his own office. Ford would argue that the role of the Freemasons in America was in fact to shift attention away from the labyrinthine anti-American plots of the Jews. Ford was later to publicly apologise for his anti-Semitic outpourings although it seems unlikely he felt any genuine regret about them.

## The P2 Scandal

Perhaps the greatest scandal relating to Freemasonry in the twentieth century centred on the Italian Masonic lodge P2 and the murder of Roberto Calvi. Formed in 1895 under the jurisdiction of the Grand Orient of Italy, P2 became increasingly corrupt, particularly under Grand Master Licio Gelli. P2 was actually dissolved as a Masonic lodge in Italy and Gelli thrown out of Freemasonry in 1976. However, he continued to operate the P2 lodge, largely as a front for criminal dealings. P2 became front-page news when, in 1982, the president of Banco Ambrosiano, Roberto Calvi, was murdered and found hanging under Blackfriars Bridge in London. He had disappeared shortly beforehand just as he had been about to give evidence in court regarding the involvement of P2 with Banco Ambrosiano and the Vatican. Originally his death was described as suicide but subsequent investigations established that he had, in fact, been murdered.

## Conspiracy Theories

In his book *Jack the Ripper: The Final Solution* the author Stephen Knight put forward the argument that the infamous serial killer, who was never caught, had been a Freemason. The murder victims were all women and the killer attacked them in a particularly vicious and savage way. Their throats were slit and their abdominal regions cut open. The infamous spate of shocking and grisly murders that took place in London's East End began on 31 August 1888 when the body of a prostitute called Mary Ann Nichols was discovered in Whitechapel.

A second murdered prostitute, identified as Annie Chapman, was found in Spitalfields on 8 September. Her uterus had been cut out by her murderer and removed from the murder scene. At this point the police were at a loss to identify the killer and the investigation, which had initially been conducted at a local level by Detective Inspector Edmund Reid, was passed on to a larger team. Three Detective Inspectors, James McWilliam, Walter Andrews and Frederick Abberline led the team. On 29 September the authorities investigating the murders received a letter, claiming to have been written by the individual responsible for the killings, who gave his name as 'Jack the Ripper'.

By the following day, there was a third murdered victim, a woman called Elizabeth Stride. In fact, the killer had struck twice on 30 September as the body of Catherine Eddowes was also found, this time in Aldgate. As with the killing of Annie Chapman, the killer had once again removed the victim's uterus and also her left kidney. Following the murder of Catherine Eddowes, a fragment of her apron was discovered in a doorway in Whitechapel. A mysterious message had been written on the wall in chalk close to where the bloodied scrap of apron was found. The strange message said: 'The Juwes are The men that Will not be Blamed for nothing.'

This vital piece of evidence was scrubbed out on the orders of Sir Charles Warren who was at that time the head of the Metropolitan Police. His justification for having the message removed was that, having translated the word 'Juwes' as simply being a misspelling of 'Jews', he was concerned that it might provoke anti-Semitic feeling and lead to violence. A second letter was sent to the police after the murders of Elizabeth Stride and Catherine Eddowes, claiming responsibility for the deaths of the two women, and once again it was signed 'Jack the Ripper'.

On 5 October 1888, the severely mutilated body of Mary Kelley was found in Spitalfields. She had been killed in bed in a boarding house in which she was staying. As the investigation escalated, an organisation called the Whitechapel Vigilance Committee was formed to try to help police apprehend the killer. On 16 October, another letter was sent to the authorities, purporting to be from the killer who was still at large. This time it was accompanied by a cardboard box that held the gruesome contents of half a human kidney. The writer claimed that he had consumed the other half of the kidney and, infamously, his letter was signed 'from hell'.

The contention of Stephen Knight and a number of other writers is that Sir Charles Warren, who was himself an important figure within Freemasonry, ordered that the strange message regarding the 'Juwes' be removed because he was seeking to protect a brother

Freemason. The graphic novel *From Hell* by Alan Moore and the subsequent film adaptation starring Johnny Depp also see the murders as being the work of a Freemason. Knight argued that what many people had regarded as an incorrect spelling of the word Jews as Juwes was in fact a direct reference to Masonic mythology. In the story of the murder of Hiram Abiff, architect of the Temple of Solomon, his killers are named as the three apprentices seeking the knowledge of a Master Mason who are called Jubela, Jubelo and Jubelum. In Masonic lore, they are, as we have seen, known collectively as the 'Juwes', a term pronounced not as 'Jews' but as 'Joo-ees'.

Stephen Knight developed a radically new theory about the Ripper murders, linking them to Freemasonry after obtaining information from Joseph Sickert. Joseph Sickert was the son of the artist Walter Sickert and claimed that his father had revealed to him hitherto unknown knowledge concerning the killings. From this information Knight reconstructed a new account of the Ripper murders. He claimed that the grandson of Queen Victoria, Prince Albert, had a relationship with a Catholic commoner called Annie Crook whom he made pregnant and subsequently married. The marriage and the child were kept secret because it was believed that such a scandal could have threatened the stability of the country. It was believed that it could have such an impact that the royal family and the government could be overthrown.

However, Knight claimed that the girl became a prostitute and revealed her secret to several other prostitutes. He claims they planned to reveal the secret marriage and child and that in desperation those in power turned to the Queen's doctor, a man named Sir William Gull, for help. Knight claims that Gull drew up a plan to kill the women. He was himself a Freemason and used his position to kill the prostitutes, relying on the aid of fellow Masons to protect him. Masons are obligated to help one another wherever possible should they find their brethren in difficulties. The nature of the killings is supposed to have reflected Masonic rituals.

However, the credibility of the story is undermined by reports that Joseph Sickert later admitted that the story had been a fiction. Critics of the theory have also argued that it seems unlikely that Gull would have been physically capable of carrying out the killings. Aged 72, the doctor is known to have already experienced a heart attack. The identity of Jack the Ripper has never been unequivocally established and some have argued that this stems largely from the fact that police methods of the time were inadequate in dealing with serial killings of this nature.

The death of the Austrian composer Wolfgang Amadeus Mozart in mysterious circumstances has also led to conspiracy theories that implicate the Freemasons. Mozart was himself a Freemason and was initiated into the lodge Zur Wahrent Eintrach or 'Lodge Beneficence' in 1785. The plot of his opera *Die*

*Zauberflote*, 'The Magic Flute', features Masonic themes and subject matter. His librettist Johan Emmanuel Schikaneder was also a Mason and suggested that Mozart produce the opera as a piece of pro-Masonic propaganda to celebrate the coronation in 1791 of the brother of Marie Antoinette, Leopold II, as Austrian Emperor. The events of the French and American Revolution had badly tarnished the image of Freemasonry and Schikaneder hoped to influence the new ruler by showing the craft in a positive light.

When Mozart died on 5 December 1791, it was rumoured that he had been poisoned. No autopsy was carried out on his body and theories soon began to circulate about the nature of his death and the possible reasons behind it. One version of events claimed that Mozart had been murdered for revealing Masonic secrets in *The Magic Flute* or that he had been a sacrifice to so-called Masonic deities. However, in a posthumous investigation held into the circumstances of his death in 2000, a group of physicians concluded that the composer had, in fact, died as a result of rheumatic fever. Rumours of a Masonic murder were effectively scotched.

More recently, Freemasonry has featured strongly in a variety of conspiracy theories concerning modern American society. It has been argued that the influence of Freemasonry can be found amongst some of the most visible symbols of the United States of America. Attention has focused on the Great Seal of the United

States that commonly appears in official contexts and on government documents. On the reverse side of the Great Seal a thirteen-stepped pyramid, surmounted by the 'Eye of Providence', is depicted. Within Masonic symbolism, the floating, disembodied eye is representative of God who, as we have seen, is often referred to as the 'Great Architect'. The eye on the Great Seal is surrounded by a 'glory', rays of light that emanate outwards. The symbol of the Eye was first incorporated as part of the Great Seal in 1782 and is grouped with the words 'Annuit Coeptis' that can be interpreted as saying America is favoured or supported by God.

At the base of the pyramid appears the words 'Novus Ordo Seclorum' declaring that America is a 'New Secular Order', formed like a pyramid of a broad base of people surmounted and watched over by the Eye of Providence. The obverse side of the Great Seal also features symbolism that can be found in Freemasonry. A 'glory' that once again symbolises God surrounds the 13 stars of the United States. Beneath the Glory is a picture of an eagle that is said to represent the spirit and carries the Arrows of War alongside the Laurel Wreath that signifies peace. The Great Seal can be found on the American one dollar bill. Some have claimed that it was President Franklin D Roosevelt, himself a Freemason, who put forward the idea in 1935 that the Great Seal appear on the one dollar bill.

It has also been argued that Freemasonry played an important role in shaping the structure and development of Mormonism. The founder of the Church of Latter Day Saints, Joseph Smith Jr, was initiated as a Freemason on 15 March 1842. Many have pointed to significant similarities between the ordinances of the Mormon priesthood and the rituals of Freemasonry, including such Masonic behaviour as the use of particular hand-grips and the swearing of oaths. Interest has also focussed on the symbolism found in the Salt Lake City Temple which many argue derives from the world of Freemasonry. The all-seeing eye and the use of the five-pointed star are examples of images and ideas that can be found in Masonic symbolism.

In fact, the architecture of the temples of The Church of Latter Day Saints, like Masonic lodges, contains many references and influences from the Biblical descriptions of the legendary Temple of Solomon. Every Mormon temple currently in use incorporates a baptismal font that is designed after the manner of the Brazen Sea that is described in 1 Kings. The fonts within Mormon temples are upheld by 12 figurines of oxen. Many important leaders within the Church of Latter Day Saints were also Freemasons, including Brigham Young, the second president of Mormonism, and his father and brothers.

It has been argued that Smith's connection to Freemasonry is borne out by the circumstances surrounding his death. He was killed in 1844 and it is said that, just before he was shot, he raised both hands in the air and cried out 'The Lord and my God'. Some have speculated that this was not simply a final appeal to God for help but was, in fact, a phrase taken from Masonry, one used when a Mason is appealing to any other Masons who might be present for their help in a time of danger.

## Skull and Bones

Recently there has been considerable speculation about the nature of the American Masonic-style 'secret society' known as the Order of Skull and Bones. The Order is based at Yale University in Connecticut and was founded in 1832 by Alphonso Taft and William Huntington Russell. Yale University has a number of similar student societies such as Wolf's Head and Scroll and Key. In the past the names of newly created members of these groups were made available through local press and they are now made known via the college newspaper.

Members of the Order of Skull and Bones are drawn from college undergraduates in a process known as being 'tapped'. Members of Skull and Bones are known as 'Bonesmen' and the society was only open to male students until 1992 when it was agreed that women could be admitted to the order. Members of the order hold meetings in what is known as the 'Bones Tomb' and, in the past, they have included individuals who went on to become presidents of the United States of America. Alleged details of the activities of the Order of Skull and Bones have emerged in a book called *Secrets of the Tomb* by the author Alexandra Robbins. It is said that members of the group refer to themselves as 'Knights' whilst non-members are termed 'Barbarians'. It has also been claimed that Bonesmen hold special society meals in the Tomb that involve the use of a silver dinner service that previously belonged to the Italian dictator Benito Mussolini. Many influential figures in American society, including George W Bush Senior, have belonged to the Skull and Bones society. In 2004, it emerged that the two Presidential Nominees, George W Bush Junior and John Kerry, had both been Bonesmen.

In recent years attempts have been made in Britain to force members of fraternal societies who occupy positions of public office to declare their membership of such groups and bodies. Tony Blair's Labour government, prompted by high-profile cases of Masons involved in illegal activities, adopted this strategy during their initial term in office at the end of the 1990s and into the millennium. However, this was disputed under European Human Rights Legislation. As a result, the government was forced to limit its policy. In 1999 the Police Service introduced a system whereby Freemasons who serve within the force can voluntarily make their membership public. There is currently no definitive listing available of individuals who are members of Freemasonic organisations.

The fears and concerns that secret societies like the Freemasons continue to provoke in the modern era is perhaps best demonstrated by the ways in which such groups are depicted in popular culture. Fascination with esoteric groups which hold secret knowledge, hidden from the general public, that provides them with an alternative view of history informs the best-selling works of the popular novelist Dan Brown. In his novel *Angel and Demons* the influence of the Masonic-style Illuminati has persisted to the present day as they seek revenge against the Roman Catholic Church. Famously, Brown precedes the events of *The Da Vinci Code* with the statement that the Priory of Sion is a real European secret society founded in 1099 and still in existence today and that its members are the guardians of the true nature of the Holy Grail.

Using an underlying theory that closely matches that of the best-selling *Holy Blood, Holy Grail* by authors Michael Baigent, Richard Leigh and Henry Lincoln, Brown's novel has a plot in which it emerges that the Grail is a metaphor for a holy blood line descended from Jesus Christ who supposedly married Mary Magdalene and had children with her. The powerful revelation of this long-kept secret, suppressed but kept alive by the Priory of Sion, threatens to topple the power of the Catholic Church. It may be a worrying thought that such paranoia and intrigue can become focussed on groups like the Freemasons because, as we have seen, it can be argued that conspiracy theories believed by such figures as Henry Ford led ultimately to the mass persecution of Masons under Hitler's Nazi regime. A more benevolent view of Freemasonry can be found in the 2004 film

*National Treasure*, starring Nicholas Cage, although once again they are portrayed as privy to a complex, hidden intrigue that has been concealed for centuries. The more mundane reality facing Freemasonry today is that its popularity is in decline, as fewer and fewer young people become members. The fading interest in joining the fraternity is in stark contrast to what appears to be a growing public obsession with the myths and legends attached to Freemasonry. In the public imagination at least, it seems likely that Freemasons will continue to be viewed as the 'men who control the world'.

# Bibliography

The Holy Bible: New Revised Standard Version, Oxford: Oxford University Press, 1995

Baigent, Michael, Leigh, Richard and Lincoln, Henry, *The Holy Blood & The Holy Grail*, London: Arrow Books, 1982

Baigent, Michael and Leigh, Richard, *The Temple and the Lodge*, London: Arrow Books, 1998

Brighton, Simon, *In Search of the Knights Templar*, London: Weidenfeld & Nicolson, 2006

Brown, Dan, *The Da Vinci Code*, London: Bantam Press, 2004

Cooper, D Jason, *Mithras: Mysteries and Initiation Rediscovered*, Newburyport, Mass: Samuel Weiser Inc, 1996

Dedopulos, Tim, *The Brotherhood*, London: Carlton Books, 2006

Hamill, John, *The Craft: A History of English Freemasonry*, London: Crucible, 1986

Harwood, Jeremy, *The Freemasons*, London: Hermes House, 2006

Jeffers, H Paul, *Freemasons: Inside the World's Oldest Secret*

*Society*, New York: Citadel Press, 2005

Johnstone, Michael, *The Freemasons: The Illustrated Book of an Ancient Brotherhood*, London: Arcturus, 2005

Knight, Christopher and Lomas, Robert, *The Hiram Key*, London: Arrow Books, 1997

Knight, Christopher and Lomas, Robert, *Turning the Hiram Key*, London: Lewis Masonic, 2005

Lomas, Robert, *The Secrets of Freemasonry: Revealing the Suppressed Tradition*, London: Robinson, 2006

MacNulty, W Kirk, *Freemasonry: Symbols, Secrets, Significance*, London: Thames & Hudson, 2006

MacNulty, W Kirk, *Freemasonry: A Journey Through Ritual and Symbol*, London: Thames & Hudson, 1994

Martin, Sean, *The Knights Templar*, London: Pocket Essentials, 2004

Mavromataki, Maria, *Greek Mythology and Religion*, Athens: Haitalis, 1997

Nicholson, Helen, *The Knights Hospitaller*, Woodbridge, Suffolk: Boydell, 2001

Porter, Lindsay, *Who Are The Illuminati?,* London: Collins & Brown, 2005

Read, Piers Paul, *The Templars*, London: Phoenix Press, 2001

# Web Pages

www.internet.lodge.org.uk
www.ugle.co.uk
www.irish-freemasons.org
www.grandlodgescotland.com
www.freemasonrywatch.org

# Index

# INDEX